CREATING STAINED GLASS LAMPSHADES

CREATING STAINED GLASS LAMPSHADES

James H. Hepburn

DOVER PUBLICATIONS, INC.
Mineola, New York

Published in Canada by General Publishing Company, Ltd., 895 Don Mills Road, 400-2 Park Centre, Toronto, Ontario M3C 1W3.
Published in the United Kingdom by David & Charles, Brunel House, Forde Close, Newton Abbot, Devon TQ12 4PU.

Bibliographical Note

This Dover edition, first published in 2001, is an unabridged, slightly corrected republication of the work originally published in 1974 by The President Press, Quincy, Massachusetts. The Dover edition includes all text and illustrations from the 1974 edition. A new Introduction to the Dover Edition has been added.

Library of Congress Cataloging-in-Publication Data

Hepburn, James H.
    Creating stained glass lampshades / by James H. Hepburn.
        p. cm.
    Originally published: Quincy, Mass. : President Press, 1974.
    ISBN 0-486-41747-6 (pbk.)
      1. Glass craft—Patterns. 2. Glass painting and staining—Patterns. 3. Glass lampshades. I. Title: Stained glass lampshades. II. Title.
TT298 H47 2001
748.5'028'2—dc21

                                              2001017201

Manufactured in the United States of America
Dover Publications, Inc., 31 East 2nd Street, Mineola, N.Y. 11501

CONTENTS

CREATING
STAINED GLASS
LAMPSHADES

CHAPTER 1

Introduction to the Dover Edition

The first edition of *Creating Stained Glass Lampshades* was published in 1974. In the original Introduction the author stated, "The demand for a book devoted entirely to instructions and illustrations of methods of constructing stained glass lampshades has existed for several years. There are a few general works in print that devote one or two chapters to this subject, but heretofore the demand for a volume devoted entirely to the subject did not warrant the expense of publishing such a work."

Since that time, there have been many books published on the subject, but most are specialized studies, excellent within the narrow limits in which they seek to treat. This book is still useful in its original purpose: to consider the general subject in a broader way, and to guide the less experienced into a gradual widening of his or her expertise.

As was stated in the original edition, this book assumes "only that the reader is slightly familiar with the general terminology used in stained glass work. The first several pages give rudimentary information and instructions in stained glass work in general and the skills and techniques are developed from this point throughout the book, building step by step into more complicated procedures and techniques."

One major change that has occurred since the original publication is the ready availability of specialized tools, such as glass grinders, glass band saws, and other moderately priced pieces of equipment, which make the seemingly tedious cutting and fitting procedures so much easier that the work can now be truly characterized more as a joyful undertaking than as a challenge.

Most of the materials and tools needed for the projects in this book are sold by stained glass hobby supply stores. They may be found listed in your classified telephone directory under *Glass—Stained and Leaded*. Many of these stores offer classes of instruction in the craft. You may also find sources of supply on the Internet. Start your search with the keywords *Stained Glass Supplies*.

Hanover, Massachusetts
September 1, 2000

CHAPTER 2

TYPES OF STAINED GLASS LAMPSHADES

There are several broad categories of stained glass lampshades. These broad categories are as follows:

1) Bent Panel Shades

Bent panel shades are generally constructed of fairly large pieces of glass which have been cut to a predetermined shape or pattern and then bent in a mold which has been placed in a furnace or kiln. These bent panel shades are produced commercially by mass production methods, and the construction of them will not be covered in this book.

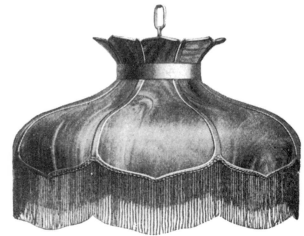

Figure 2-1

2) Simple Flat Panel Shades With Lead Cames

For the most part, these are the lampshades which are sold as pre-cut lampshade kits in certain craft and hobby shops. They are rather simple to make, and the stained glass craftsman can usually create them without difficulty and with very little instruction. They are, for the most part, rather common, although some very beautiful examples are seen from time to time.

Figure 2-2

3) Multi-Pieced Leaded Glass Lampshades Made by the Lead Came Method

Not too many examples are seen of this type of lampshade. Quite often they consist of skirts, which contain many pieces of glass, and a body or upper portion which has relatively few pieces, or a simple grid. Any shade made in this fashion must be cemented after it is built in order to stiffen it.

Figure 2-3

2

4) Multi-Pieced Leaded Glass Lampshades Made by the Copper Foil Method

These lampshades cover the widest variety of shapes, sizes, designs, and colors of any type of lampshade. Almost without exception, the lampshades made by the Tiffany Studios were made by the copper foil method.

5) Lanterns, Candle Chimneys, Cylinders, and Similar types

These are essentially boxes or cylinders made of leaded glass. They are usually constructed with lead came, and are almost always extremely simple in their construction.

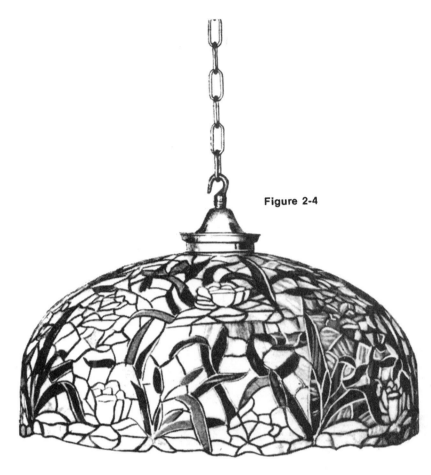

Figure 2-4

6) Lampshades Made Using Lamp Frames

These are a variation of the panel shade.

There are many other varieties of lampshades using stained glass, but they are mostly variations of these major classifications. In this book we will discuss methods and procedures of making all of these types with the exception of the bent panel shades.

Figure 2-5

3

CHAPTER 3

THE BASICS

Location of the Work

Because of the considerable length of time required to complete some of the lampshade projects, some thought should be given to the location of the work area. The preferable spot would be in a cellar or in a workshop at a bench which can remain undisturbed for extended lengths of time. The top of the work area should be of wood (preferably plywood). Failing this, the next best arrangement would be to have a piece of plywood at least 30 inches by six feet which can be picked up in its entirety and stored away between sessions. This workboard can be used in the kitchen or some other room in the house, and the surrounding areas and floor covered with newspaper to prevent damage to any of the furnishings because of errant pieces of glass or droplets of hot solder.

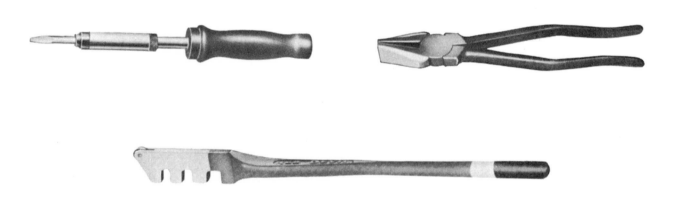

Figure 3-1. Specialized tools required for doing stained glass lampshade work. Soldering Iron, Sharp Glass Cutters, and Glass Pliers.

Materials

If you contemplate continuing activities in the stained glass lampshade field, you should acquire the following tools and equipment:

Soldering Iron & Tips	Pattern Paper (Brown Grocery Bags will do)
Glass Pliers	Carbon Paper
Glass Cutters	Scissors
Straight Edge for	Ruler for taking measurements
use with a glass cutter	and drawing straight lines

4

In addition to these tools and equipment, the following items are required which are consumed or become part of the lampshade.

Glass   Copper Foil   Flux

Lead Came   Solder   Kerosene for lubricating the glass cutter

Copper Sulphate for darkening the color of the solder

The electrical part of the lampshade requires other common tools which are usually found around the house.

If you have never worked with glass before, or if you have never done any stained glass work, the following part of the chapter is very important because it sets forth the basic skills used in working with these materials. If you have already worked with stained glass, and have mastered the craft of cutting glass to pattern and soldering lead and copper foil, you may skip over to the next chapter.

Leaded or Stained Glass in General

So-called "Stained Glass Lampshades" are, in reality, lampshades made from pieces of colored glass bound together with a metal strip which encases the edge of every piece of glass in the lampshade. Most lampshades, and particularly, any lampshade of high quality, utilize opal or opalescent glass. Opal or opalescent glass is colored glass which is heavily translucent because of the materials used in the manufacture of the glass. The majority of opal or opalescent glasses are marbleized in appearance and consist of some two to five colors of glass mixed together. When the glass is illuminated, as in a lampshade, the very sharp divisions between the colors are softened, and the various layers of colors which occur one above the other blend together so that the effect is totally different from the effect seen when the lampshade is not illuminated.

Figure 3-2. Lampshade work in progress showing metal strips between small pieces of glass. [Courtesy Dan Suter, Rochester, N.Y.]

Success in manipulating the colors, and intelligent choice of color based on experience and study of the properties of the glass add a tremendous plus to the beauty of the finished project.

No color photograph can truly do justice to a stained glass lampshade that has been created by an expert.

Some people prefer lampshades made with a glass with less translucency than opal or opalescent glass. They use rolled cathedral glass, or antique glass (a term meaning merely that the glass was manufactured by the antique method of glassblowing). Great care must be exercised in designing lamps with glasses such as these, because the light source or bulb is completely visible through the glass which is almost transparent. Special bulbs may be required.

Figure 3-3. Opalescent glass completely obscures the bulb, and gives a rich, deep, tone to the entire lampshade.

Various methods are used for holding the glass into place and various methods are used in structuring the lampshade, but in general, the term "leading" is close enough to actuality to be usable. A leaded glass lampshade consists of glass which is bound together with lead channeling which is soldered at its intersection, or it is bound together with channels of very thin copper which is covered with solder. Solder contains up to 50% lead, and the process of covering the copper foil is called "leading" in this case.

Figure 3-4. This lampshade requires an antique filament lightbulb of very low wattage to prevent too much glare.

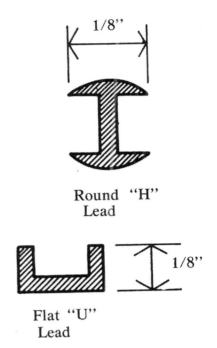

1/8"

Round "H" Lead

1/8"

Flat "U" Lead

Figure 3-5. These two basic shapes are the ones used in almost all lampshade work which utilizes the lead came method.

The Mechanics of Making Leaded Glass Shades

The skills required in working with stained glass whether you are making lampshades or windows are the same. You must learn how to cut glass with a cutter. You must not only master the skill of cutting glass in a straight line, but also of cutting glass into curves of various degrees of complexity.

The second skill required is that of soldering metal with a soldering iron. Diligent practice in soldering will quickly enable you to produce acceptable, passable work. A certain touch is required to produce excellent work, and there are craftsman who have been engaged in stained glass work for many years who have not really mastered the art of making a perfect solder joint. But then again, none of us is perfect.

The other skills required in making stained glass lampshades are normal, everyday manual skills which can be developed quickly if they are not already possessed. A certain degree of common sense is also an asset, and of course, a check list of other virtues should certainly include patience, persistence, and objectiveness in viewing one's finished work.

Cutting the Glass

The first major obstacle to overcome if you intend to invest any time or money in stained glass lampshade work is to master the technique of glass cutting. Before making a major outlay for materials, supplies, tools and books on the subject, you should really determine whether or not you will want to devote the time and effort needed to learn how to cut glass. Most hardware stores that handle window glass sell it cut to size. They usually have a glass cutting board or a table for cutting window panes to size for customers, and beneath this apparatus they usually keep a waste receptacle into which the proprietor discards the various sized strips of glass which have been cut out from the customer's window pane.

It is highly unlikely that the nice man at the hardware store will object to giving you these scraps free of charge. This waste material is in reality a difficult material to dispose of easily because of its weight and obvious hazards. You should have no difficulty in taking more than enough of this scrap glass to enable you to practice glass cutting for many hours. Practice all sorts of ridiculous cuts and curves so that you have mastered the technique thoroughly in theory, and have a rudimentary idea of what to expect when working with glass which costs anywhere from $3.00 to $5.00 per square foot.

In all honesty, you must understand that window glass is very soft, and the ability to cut window glass is merely a step in the right direction. Opal and opalescent glass, and most cathedral glasses, are very hard surfaced glasses and usually much more pressure must be brought upon the glass cutter in order to make the score upon the surface. The knowledge, however, that you can actually cut glass is a very comforting one to have before you invest relatively large sums of money into something which may be only an experiment.

If you happen to be a very personable individual, you may even persuade the nice man at the hardware store to show you how to cut glass.

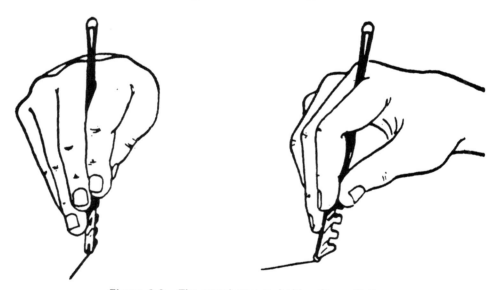

Figure 3-6. The usual way to hold a Glass Cutter.

You will note that the illustration shows the proper way to hold a glass cutter. This position is used by the vast majority of people who cut glass professionally. There are other variations and different grips in use, and the adherents of these other positions claim superiority for their method. Inasmuch as there has apparently never been a tournament or an adjudication sponsored by any official body to determine the correct way to hold a glass cutter, we will rest upon our statement that the one in the picture is the one that you should use. the only variation of this position would be to turn the glass cutter 180° so that the notches of the cutter are facing away from you. You will find that in many instances this is preferable because it allows you to see the actual contact point between the wheel and the glass which is desirable when you are cutting intricate patterns using a pattern stencil laid upon the glass.

Figure 3-7. General position of body and arm when cutting glass from larger sheets.

The glass must be placed on a flat surface which has been brushed absolutely clean of all debris, grit, or anything else which might scratch the glass. If you are merely cutting a straight line in the glass, such as you might wish to do to remove a small rectangular piece from a larger rectangular piece preparatory to cutting some small pieces from it, you would hold the glass cutter in contact with the glass (as shown in the illustration) at the edge of the glass furthest from you, bear down upon the glass with approximately 10 pounds of pressure, and being sure to hold the glass cutter vertically at all times, draw it toward you. The noise made by the glass cutter against the glass is unmistakable. It is the sound of glass being scratched or crushed, which in reality is what you are doing. You are rupturing the surface of the glass causing it to weaken along a predetermined path. At this point, the glass has not been cut but the score has been made. The actual operation to separate the two pieces of glass consists of bending the glass in such a manner as to put a strain on the glass along the path of the score, which is the weakest part of the glass. If this is done properly, the glass will separate along the score and the cut will have been achieved.

This is a general, theoretical description of what occurs when glass is cut. We will now look into it in a little more detail.

9

The glass cutters in use today are almost exclusively steel-wheeled cutters. The wheel is usually 7/32" in diameter and is mounted on a bronze bearing which is impinged with oil. The bearing or axle is held in place in a zinc or steel casting which forms the body and handle of the cutter. Although the tool is an inexpensive one, abusing it or damaging it needlessly is wasteful. It is possible to get thousands of running feet of use from one glass cutter if it is maintained properly.

Maintaining a glass cutter properly consists of the following points:

1) The glass cutter should be dipped in kerosene to lubricate it occasionally. The lubricant also serves as a coolant to prevent the wheel from heating up and becoming prematurely dull. The easiest way to take care of the kerosene supply is to place a small amount in the bottom of an empty tin can and drop a pad of gauze or small folded cloth into the bottom. The folded cloth prevents the wheel from coming in contact with the bottom of the tin can if it is dropped into the can accidently. In no instances should turpentine or paint thinner be used as a lubricant for a glass cutter. Turpentine is a solvent which can disolve oil, and it will disolve the oil which is impinged in the bearing of the cutter and cause early failure. If you cannot get kerosene, use the very lightest oil you can possibly obtain. Three-In-One oil or sewing machine oil are very light oils.

2) Do not drop the glass cutter, and be careful that the glass cutter is not kept in a tool drawer where the wheel may come in contact with other tools or objects which might dull it.

3) Never retrace or go over a cut or a score in the glass once it has been made. If you attempt to score a piece of glass and the score mark is not complete or portions of the line have been skipped, move your straight edge or pattern away from the mark and make an entirely new cut. Going over a score that has been made has two effects on the wheel. It can damage the cutting edge of the wheel and it can bend the axle or bearing.

4) Do not bear down harder on the glass than is necessary. Very little experience will reveal to you the amount of pressure needed to make a score upon the glass just deep enough to do the job.

There are glass cutters produced using wheels of tungsten carbide steel. The price is usually five or six times as much as for the price of a standard glass cutter. No claim is made that the cutter is sharper than the other cutters, but it is claimed that they outlast the regular glass cutter many times more than the additional cost would indicate.

The mechanics of making scores or cuts in the glass and breaking the glass are as follows:

A. Cutting the Glass

1. **If a straight line is desired,** a straight edge should be used as a guide along which the glass cutter is drawn. In lampshade work, there is very little straight line work required, except in some of the very simple ones, or in making grid patterns.

2. **Cutting to Pattern.** There are several ways of cutting glass to a pattern. They are as follows:

a. When the pattern has been cut into the individual pieces called stencils, you may put the individual stencil underneath the glass and follow the lines with your glass cutter. It is obvious that this will not work with opal or opalescent glass, but only with the more transparent glasses.

b. You can lay the individual stencil upon the glass and cut around the pattern the same way you would if you were tracing around the pattern with a pencil.

c. You may put the stencil on the glass and trace around it with a china or glass marking crayon. You can then follow this crayon mark with your glass cutter.

3. **Breaking the Glass.** There are various ways of breaking the glass, and all of them are useful and can be utilized from time to time. When the piece to be broken off is fairly large, it can be broken the same way you would break a soda cracker. (See Figure 3-9.)

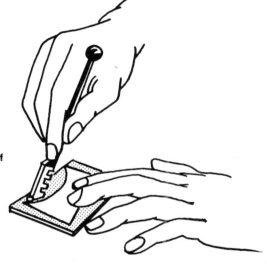

Figure 3-8. **The usual method of cutting glass from paper stencils.**

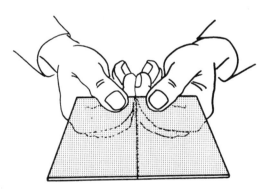

Figure 3-9. **Snapping the cut.**

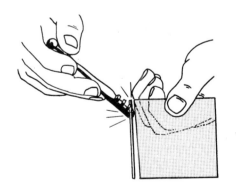

Figure 3-10. **Using the notch of the glass cutter to break the cut.**

Narrow strips can be removed using the notch of your glass cutter as a breaker. (See Figure 3-10.) If the glass resists when you attempt breaking it by hand, the cut may be started by tapping the underside of the glass. The end of a ball end glass cutter is useful for this, although any similar object can be used. (See Figure 3-11.)

11

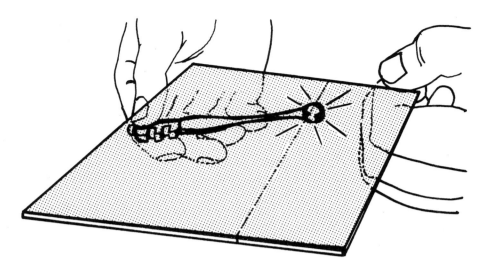

Figure 3-11. Using the ball on the end of the glass cutter to start the break.

The most useful tool in breaking glass for lampshade work is the glass pliers. (See Figure 3-12.) These tools have wide jaws and the faces of the jaws are not serated, but rather are smooth. They grip the glass firmly and apply pressure evenly so that small pieces can be broken off. They can also be used for chewing away parts of the glass that did not break evenly or making inside notches where the danger of spoiling the glass would preclude the attempt of making an ordinary cut.

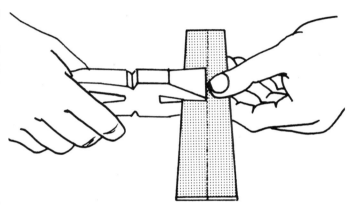

Figure 3-12. Using the glass pliers to break off pieces too narrow to be broken by the fingers.

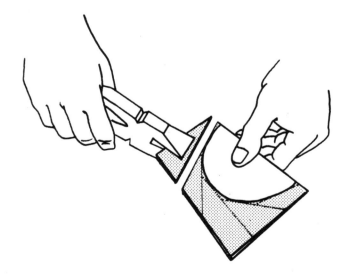

Figure 3-13. Method of cutting curves of small radius showing several cuts required.

12

4. The Technique of Cutting Sharp Curves. The depth of the score in the glass is merely a slight weakening of the glass, but practice will soon show you that a sharp corner or a curve of a small radius will usually be ignored by the glass when you attempt to break out your cut piece. Breaking out intricate patterns cannot be done all in one fell swoop. Any curves of small radii must first be scored into a series of short segments.(See Figure 3-13.) These short segments should carry over to the edge of the glass in each instance so that when you snap off the waste pieces they are guided away from the piece you are trying to save. Quite often a pattern piece requires ten or twelve cuts in order to produce the piece that is going to be used. Even after the piece has been finally cut you will notice many small protrusions and high points on the edge that will have to be chewed off with your glass pliers.

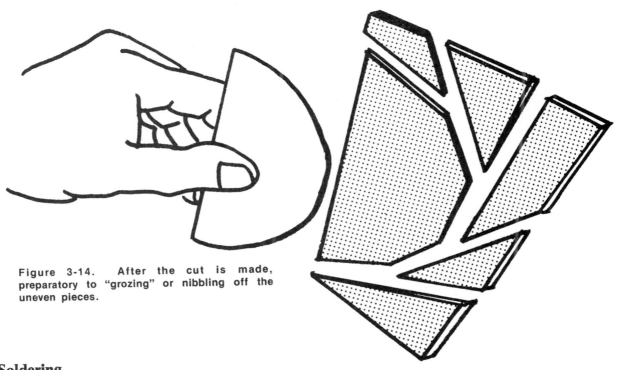

Figure 3-14. After the cut is made, preparatory to "grozing" or nibbling off the uneven pieces.

B. Soldering

Techniques of soldering vary, but one of the cardinal rules is this: **To produce good work you must have good equipment.** You must have an iron of a size and wattage suited to the job. For lampshade work in general, an iron should be of the type used in industry, rather than the types that are produced for hobby work. The reason for this is that lampshade work requires long periods of continuous soldering, and industrial type irons are built for this type work.

The preferable iron is one that is light in weight. There are many professional irons that weigh almost one pound, and are made primarily for soldering iron, steel and other materials where wide faces of metal present themselves to be soldered. An iron with a 5/8ths or 3/4" wide tip is required for heavier work such as this. In lampshade work, however, most of the soldering is required on areas only 1/8 to 1/4" wide. It is obvious, then, that larger irons would be a hindrance rather than an asset.

13

We recommend, therefore, an iron in the 40 to 80 watt range with a replaceable tip shaped like a pyramid.

Any iron that is used should have a complete set of instructions with it. These instructions give full descriptions of the steps needed to maintain the iron in good working order. Failure to read and follow these instructions leads quickly to the ruination of your iron.

Figure 3-15. Usual soldering iron tip for use in stained glass lampshade work.

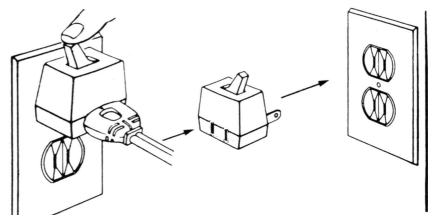

Figure 3-16. Inexpensive cord switch for regulating the heat of the soldering iron.

If possible, you should select an iron that is equipped with tips that are plated. These plated tips have a copper core. They are plated with iron, and then plated with an alloy to reduce corrosion and pitting. During use, they need only to be wiped on a damp sponge to keep them shiny and efficient.

60/40 solder melts at 375°F. Many irons reach 800 to 1200°F. It is therefore unnecessary and harmful to allow the soldering iron to be plugged in continuously. If the iron you purchase does not have a switch, you should equip the outlet with a switch so that the iron can be unplugged when it becomes obvious that the heat is far in excess of what is required to melt the solder.

Flux

A flux is an agent which is applied to the metal before the solder is put on. It is used to help the two metals fuse together by preventing oxidation. In lead particularly, the surface of the lead is continuously combining with the oxygen in the air to form lead oxide. This lead oxide forms a film upon the surface of the lead, and solder in many instances will not adhere to it. The flux cuts through this surface film and wherever the flux has been applied the solder will follow.

By far the most popular flux for use in stained glass work is oleic acid. This is an animal tallow, and it is non-caustic. Under most conditions it does not cause undesirable reactions on the skin, nor does inhalation of the fumes usually cause any appreciable side effects. These two statements should be modified to the extent that there is sure to be someone, someplace who is affected by oleic acid. Suffice it to say that oleic acid has been used as a flux in stained glass work for several centuries, and although there are many other fluxes available, its continued usage indicates that it is non-caustic. Even so, if you have any misgivings about its use, rubber gloves should be worn.

There are paste fluxes which are available in the local hardware store. These are applied with stiff brushes. They contain zinc chloride, and contain a definite warning label on every can. These paste fluxes tend to spatter when the heat is applied to the area and they create a cleaning problem.

Muriatic acid which is sold under the general name "Tinners' Fluid" at most hardware stores is a flux that is used when something very strong is required such as instances where the steel fixture strap has to be soldered to the lampshade. Muriatic acid is a diluted form of hydrochloric acid. It is harmful to the skin and extremely poisonous if swallowed.

Solder

By far the most preferable solder for use in stained glass work is called 60/40 solid core solder.

Solder is an alloy of tin and lead. The melting point of solder depends entirely upon the percent of the two metals used.

Tin melts at 450°F, and lead melts at 621°F. When the two are combined however, the melting point can be as low as 361°F. The following table illustrates the melting points of the various alloys.

Percent Tin	Percent Lead	Melting Point
0	100	621°F
10	90	572°F
30	70	496°F
40	60	460°F
50	50	421°F
60	40	375°F
63	37	361°F*

*Lowest possible melting point of the alloy.

As the amount of tin is increased and the lead reduced from the 63/37 combination, the melting point begins to increase again until, at 100% tin, melting point reaches 450°F.

It is understandable that if you are attempting to solder two pieces of lead together whose melting point is 621°F, you will want to use solder with as low a melting point as possible. This solder is the 60/40 combination available commercially.

Cores

Solder is available as solid core or acid core. Solid core solder is the only kind which should be considered in stained glass work.

Soldering Techniques

The following are the most common difficulties encountered in soldering and account for most of the failures:

1) The iron is not hot enough to melt the solder. 60/40 solder melts at 375°F. 50/50 solder melts at 421°F. Other combinations of solder such as 40/60 melt at higher temperatures. It can be seen then that if the iron does not attain a temperature substantially higher than this, either the solder will not melt, or it will melt imperfectly and cause the solder joint to be lumpy and misshapen. Soldering irons used in this type work must be of high enough wattage to reach temperatures in excess of that needed to melt solder.

2) The soldering iron tip was not clean. Soldering iron tips which are unplated require regular attention to maintain them at the height of their efficiency. An ordinary copper tip will accumulate corrosion as a by-product of the soldering. This corrosion is a combination of impurities in the solder, and residue from the flux. It must be removed periodically, otherwise the tips will become completely covered with a hard crust, which will prevent the heat from radiating from the tip and consequently making it impossible to melt solder.

Regular shop practice requires that the soldering iron be kept coated with solder at all times, and particularly as the soldering is being finished, the iron should be coated with solder so that it is "tinned" completely when it has cooled off.

This corrosion has to be removed from the tip occasionally by the use of a file or by sandpaper. This is why we recommend using a plated tip, which although considerably more expensive, makes it unnecessary to spend so much time in maintainance of the soldering iron tip. The plated tips merely require wiping on a wet sponge to remove the accretion from time to time.

3) The lead or copper which is to be soldered was not completely cleaned, or no flux was used. Any metal will tarnish from exposure to the air. Lead will tarnish more rapidly than most metals, and if lead has been exposed to the air for any length of time it takes on a definite discoloration which is apparent to the eye, and solder will merely lie on the surface and not actually fuse with the lead. The metal must be clean, and if any tarnish is apparent to the eye, the metal should be scraped or rubbed with steel wool, and sufficient flux used to cause a good union.

Types of Solder Joints

In general, the most desirable joint is the one that is the most inobtrusive. In lead came, only enough solder should be used to actually attach the two pieces together.

Larger amounts of solder inevitably detract from the appearance of the piece. Larger amounts of solder also require more work in the application, and are more difficult to blend in later when you are trying to apply an antiquing solution. The solder joint used in leaded glass lampshade work when lead came is being used should be as flat as possible.

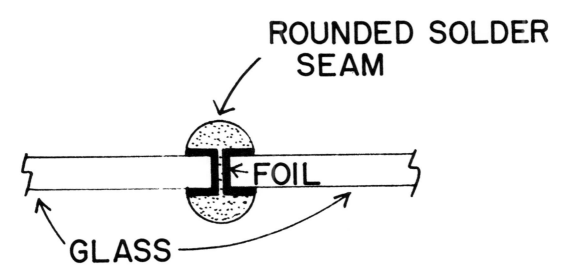

Figure 3-17. Preferred shape of solder joint in copper foil work.

In copper foil work, the most preferable appearance is that of a rounded, beaded line. It is obvious that if the temperature of the soldering iron is allowed to reach the higher levels this will be impossible. The iron almost inevitably should be equipped with a switch on the cord so that the temperature can be regulated by turning the iron off and on. Better still, a wattage controller can be used and set for a pre-determined setting which will keep the iron at a constant temperature. The difficulty in running joints so that the joint has the appearance of a rounded or beaded strip is that the solder, if too hot, will be liquified to such a state that it will run between the metal and through to the other side before any buildup of solder can be attained.

Summary

Before attempting any large scale lampshade project, and before investing any appreciable sum of money in materials and tools, it would be best to first try your hand at glass cutting and soldering. The results of these experiments will determine which of the projects in the book will be within your scope.

CHAPTER 4

ABOUT PATTERNS

Unless one is quite familiar with stained glass lampshades, and has seen many of them, an attempt to build a lampshade may not get much further than the desire to do so, because of the absence of plans or patterns. A good pattern is extremely important in lampshade building. An unfortunate choice of pattern or a pattern which presents so many mechanical problems that it would be difficult to build even for an expert will do no more than discourage the amateur and stifle any initiative that he may have originally had.

I Ideas for Lampshade Patterns

More so than at any time within recent memory, stained glass lampshades are commonly seen in restaurants and public buildings in larger cities. Within the past several years newspapers, and magazines have increased their interest in the stained glass craft to a noticeable degree. Articles are written about stained glass lampshades from the viewpoint of the home craftsman or the antique collector, and illustrations are fairly common. In addition, many of the home decorating magazines show stained glass lampshades used in interior decorating schemes, and a fair portfolio of illustrations can be gleaned from back issues of these. We have noticed that the fashions in magazine and book illustrations have changed enough in the past several years so that some of the furnishings in story illustrations show stained glass lampshades.

There are also textbooks on the subject, and there are many firms who specialize in stained glass lampshade kits who sell stained glass lampshade patterns.

Any of these sources should be good ones provided they depict lampshades that have actually been built, and which are not merely figments of the imagination of someone not familiar with construction techniques.

II Shapes of Stained Glass Lampshades

Stained glass lampshades (exclusive of lanterns, lamp chimneys and the like) are usually constructed so that the upper part of the shade is small and as the sides descend, they widen, so that the general over-all shape is that of an inverted bowl or dish. This shape may consist of flat planes or it may consist of curved planes. Some shades consist of large quantities of small flat planes which form a grid work, and the pieces are so small that the lampshade appears to be actually curved. Some typical lampshade shapes are shown in the various illustrations accompanying this chapter.

a. Obviously, the easiest lampshade to construct is one consisting of flat panels of a relatively large size which are combined together to form a pyramid or modified pyramid shape. These lampshades may or may not have several tiers, and may have aprons or skirts. The work can be done on a flat surface, and then the various panels can be assembled.

Figure 4-1. A simple globe shape.

Figure 4-2. A modified cone shape.

b. The next easiest to construct is the conical shape, because although there are curves involved, they occur only on one plane. The patterns for a cone can be designed upon a flat drawing table. Even though the pattern is curved on one plane, when the pattern paper is laid upon the actual shape or form which is to be used to build the shade, the pattern paper can be trimmed so that it is actually the exact size of the surface of the cone. When the pattern paper is lifted off of the form and put onto the drawing table, it is a relatively simple matter to design the pattern.

Figure 4-3. A bell shape.

Figure 4-4. A mushroom shape.

19

c. The Globe, the Bell or the Dome Shape. These shapes are by far the most difficult to pattern. The main difficulty lies in the fact that the surface upon which the lampshade is to be built is curved on two planes. The difficulty in depicting a pattern which curves on two planes is obvious when one takes an ordinary sheet of writing paper and tries to wrap it around any sphere such as a vase, basketball, fishbowl, etc. It is possible to bend the paper in one direction, but when the paper must also be bent in the other direction it is obvious that some accommodation must be made.

Figure 4-5. A hexagon with flat panels.

There are two ways to handle this problem. One way is to segment the pattern, which means cutting slits, darts or gussets into the pattern so that the pattern takes on the shape of the map of the world in a geography text book. See Illustration 4-6. This seems simple enough, but the actual mechanics of it are quite involved, and the work required to make the original master pattern is quite often more than the work in actually drawing the design. After the master pattern is made and slit so that it can be pinned upon the form, the entire drawing must be laid out while the pattern is on the form itself so that the pieces of the pattern which bridge over the slits in the pattern can be accurately drawn.

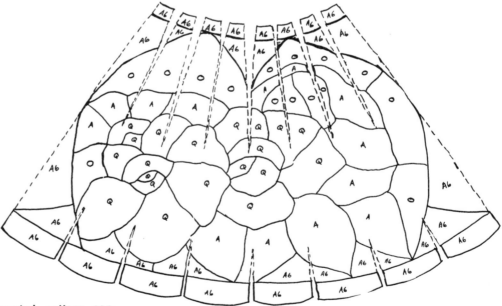

Figure 4-6. A segmented pattern consisting of three repeats.

20

The second method is the one most used by craftsmen who make their own designs. The form is used as the drawing board, and the design of the lampshade is actually drawn onto the form. The pattern work, the numbers, and the color codes are also drawn onto the form. The stencils are actually developed from this reference piece by piece. The pieces are traced off using tracing paper, and transferred onto stencil paper, and then the glass is cut. At most, this is a very tedious process but if the lampshade to be built is to be the only one of its kind, the time spent in this exercise is very likely to be no more than would be spent in any other method. It will be noted that any combination of shapes fall into the above three categories. If any portion of the pattern must be bent on two planes, the pattern cannot be laid out on a flat surface without cutting slits or gussets into it.

III Translating or Adapting

Quite often the lamp which one sees or the design which one admires most is built into a lampshade which is unsuitable in size or shape. In other instances, the lampshade one wishes to build is entirely too complicated in the shape that is shown. It might be much easier to build as a flat panelled shade or a shade in a conical shape.

The most likely need to adaptation occurs when one possesses a shade form and wishes to re-use it, but other patterns of the size required for the shade form are not available. In these instances, if one possesses a shade form and one also possesses a set of patterns for the lampshade that has already been built on the shade form, one may merely produce a set of blank pattern papers of the correct size to fit the shade form, and fill in the blank pattern paper with the pattern adapted from the photograph, illustration or other source which one wishes to copy.

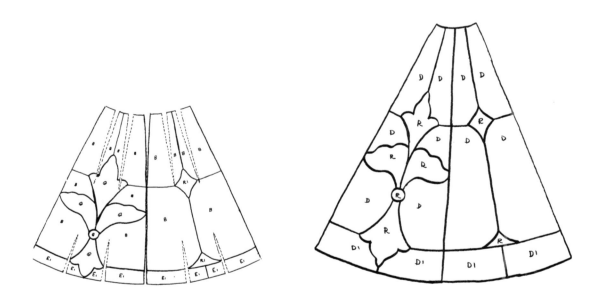

Figure 4-7. Two patterns of the same design, but modified to fit different shapes. One, a 16" globe the other an 18" cone.

21

It can be seen that this might be much easier to describe than to actually accomplish. This may be true, but there are people who possess a faculty for this sort of thing, and if one cannot grasp the fundamentals at first, some assistance from others might be called for.

It should be borne in mind that the pattern for a lampshade represents very little investment for materials. If, at some point in the proceedings you have the feeling that the lampshade should not be built, it would be far better to discard the pattern and begin again than to go ahead and translate the paper pattern into an actual undertaking which might not get much further than the glass cutting stage.

In any case, the obvious rule to follow is that if the pattern paper cannot be attached to the lamp form in such a way that it adequately covers the form snugly, it should not be used for making stencils or any other work on that particular lampshade.

IV Mechanics

Earlier in the chapter we alluded to two methods of stained glass lampshade pattern making. In one instance, the pattern was designed on the lampshade form. In the other, paper patterns were made in one way or another.

In either method, the original design work done in pencil in a rather tentative way. After an agreement is reached as to the final design and pattern the lines are gone over heavily to give them definition.

After the point is reached, the differences begin.

Developing Working Drawings and Stencils from a Pattern drawn on a Lampshade Form

This exercise is somewhat similar to that of making a rubbing of an existing lampshade. When one makes a rubbing of an existing lampshade, one does only small patches of it at one time. Soft paper such as construction paper is taped into place on the lamp------never more than a 6" x 6" piece------and a stick of charcoal or black crayon is rubbed all over the paper to transfer the raised design of the metalwork onto the paper.

As you can see, one might make a rubbing of a complete lampshade this way, and tape the resulting pieces together in such a way that one might almost have a complete working pattern except for the fact that if the lampshade is curved on two planes, one is still faced with the dilemma of depicting a curved pattern upon a flat surface.

If one is merely making a rubbing of a lampshade however, one still must think of what to use for a lampshade form. In this case we have a pattern but we have no form upon which to build the lampshade. In the earlier part of this sub-section we referred to the case where we have a lampshade form with a pattern upon it, and need a way to remove the pattern from the form so that we can make the patterns into stencils. The relationship between these two problems is apparent. We must use tracing paper, or onion skin paper, to remove small portions of the pattern from the form by tracing over them. Using carbon paper beneath the tracing paper, we must transfer the small portions to heavy pattern paper from which we can make stencils and thereby cut the glass.

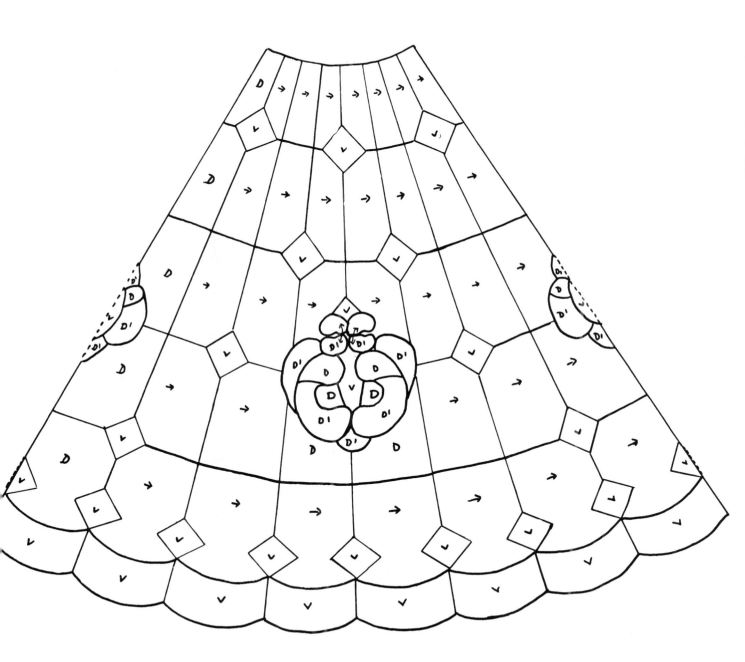

Figure 4-8. A pattern with 6 repeats.

The temptation is to make abstractions of large patches of the lampshades pattern from the form, but this always leads to distortion of the dimensions of the pieces, this in turn leads to the stretching of the glass-metal assembly when it is laid flat, resulting in work that does not fit upon the pattern within the lines allotted to it.

Once these problems are understood, work can progress the way it will be described in any of the chapters yet to come.

The Mechanics of Making a Pattern on a Flat Surface

If the surface of the form consists of flat panels or is conical in shape so that the pattern only bends on one plane, the paper can be trimmed to the exact size required and placed on the workboard and all of the designing can be done on the flat surface. There is little need to describe the mechanics of designing and filling the areas with the subject matter of the lampshade.

Repeats

Stained glass lampshades usually have patterns which repeat. A very few of them have non-repeating patterns but the usual number of repeats in a floral shade is 3 or 4. Lampshades with two repeats are seen occasionally, and lampshades exist with as many as 6 repeats. These latter types with multiple repeats are usually geometrical designs, or stylized designs of other subjects which lend themselves to a geometrical treatment.

From the standpoint of the builder, the more repeats there are in a lampshade, the less work there will be as far as stencil cutting and designing are concerned.

In designing repeats into a pattern, care must be taken so that the dividing line between the portions of the design which repeat are not artificial looking or over-delineated.

Making Stencils

Although stencil making will be described further from time to time in the other chapters of this book, they will be described in conjunction with specific projects.

In general, stencils are the small pieces of patterns that have been cut up for use as guides for cutting the pieces of glass.

Any pattern, once it has been designed and drawn accurately should be reserved as a reference drawing, and additional drawings should be made from it on heavy paper using carbon paper. These other drawings are the drawings that should be used in the actual work. One of them can be used as a locator upon which to stack the glass once it has been cut. This drawing insures that all of the glass has been cut. It gives a place for storing it so that it is readily accessible. It also prevents the various pieces from being mixed.

The most legible copy should be the one to cut into stencils. The stencils may be cut from the drawing with a pair of scissors or with an "Exacto" knife. In the case of lampshades being made with lead cames, however, a double-bladed tool must be used to make an allowance for the width of the lead. This is discussed more fully in Chapter 9.

These stencils, which should be numbered and color coded before they are cut apart, should be sorted by color and put into separate envelopes.

Most craftsmen retain all of the drawings they used on a specific project. This includes the stencils and the actual drawing that was used as the working drawing.

The Relationship Between the Working Drawing and the Form

Obviously, it is a rather chancy thing to build the lampshade on the form without any reference point. Most craftsmen use carbon paper and one of the copies of the drawing to transfer the pattern onto the form to make sure that when the entire pattern is depicted upon the form that all of the space is filled, and that none of it is filled by more than one part of the pattern.

It is absolutely necessary to do something like this. It is impossible to build under the conditions demanded in lampshade work and expect that when one moves around the circumference of the lamp form, and arrives at the starting point, he will have just the right space left to take the last pieces of glass.

Summary

Be meticulous in your choice of pattern and very careful in laying it out and making your working drawings. Much time and much disappointment can be avoided if you pay close attention to this phase of the work.

CHAPTER 5

A CANDLE CHIMNEY

Candle Chimneys are relatively simple to construct. They require no form, and they are usually four-sided box-like affairs which require only minimum amount of glass cutting and soldering.

The design we have chosen admits of many possibilities for variations, and the very simple instructions allow for much deviation and give plenty of opportunities for personal interpretations.

The Pattern

Candle chimneys usually utilize random cuts of glass which are combined in a "stacked" array in a multi-colored assortment. Some candle chimneys are hexagonal, and some are octagonal. The pattern we have decided upon for this chapter is four-sided, but the technique or general instructions can be adapted to chimneys with other numbers of sides. The candle chimney shown is 8" high. In order to get a good proportion, the width of the various glasses used in the chimney will be 3".

In the illustration, the candle chimney has very few pieces of glass on each side. This can be varied to suit, but in any event, a preliminary drawing on a full scale would be helpful.

Making allowances for lead joints, the total measurement of glass plus lead on each side of the candle chimney should be 7¾". This means that when you have cut your glass to the random width and inserted the lead between them and the entire combination is nailed onto the workbench, the distance from the outside edge of each end piece of glass should be 7¾".

Figure 5-1. Candle Chimneys allow for a wide variation of design possibilities.

Lead Came

The lead came used in a candle chimney can be any number of combinations, but in our illustration we have chosen an "H" lead with a 3/16th" face for the intermediate divisions, and a 90° angle lead for the four corners plus the upper and lower rims. The upper and lower rims take up ¼".

Figure 5-2. 90° angle lead came.

You should lay out the glass and lead for each of the four sides so that each of the four groups of glass adds up to 7¾". Change the glass around as you wish, to make the most pleasing arrangement.

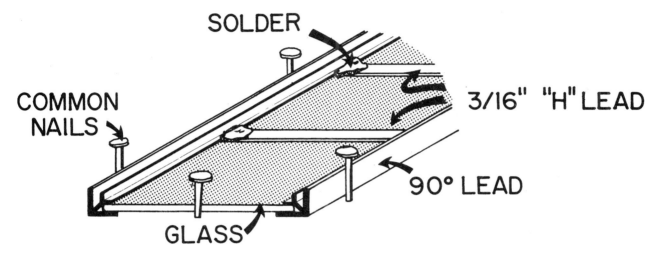

Figure 5-3. Assembling the first side.

Assembling The Panels

Working on a scrap of board or plywood, assemble one side of the chimney as shown holding the glass and lead in place with small nails. (Figure 5—3.) Assemble the glass and lead snugly. The glass and lead stacks should protrude approximately 1/8th" beyond each end of the side leads. In order to accomplish this, the side leads should be cut 7½" long. When the stack of glass plus the intermediate leads are put into this arrangement, they will total 7¾", and the corner lead, being 7 1/2" will be 1/8" short of covering the edge of the glass stack.

Solder the intersections where the "H" lead and the right angle lead join. Remove the nails, turn the entire assembly over and solder the corresponding spots on the other side. This procedure should be followed again to make side number two of the chimney.

On the third side, you will not use right angle lead along the edges but you will utilize the right angle lead from side number one and side number two and hold them in position with weights or supports as shown. The soldering should be done on the inside as before, and then the assembly should be turned over and soldered on the outside.

27

The fourth side of the candle chimney is built by turning the entire assembly over and sliding the glass and lead into the open groove of the remaining open right-angle leads from either end of the chimney. When they are in place, they should be soldered both inside and out.

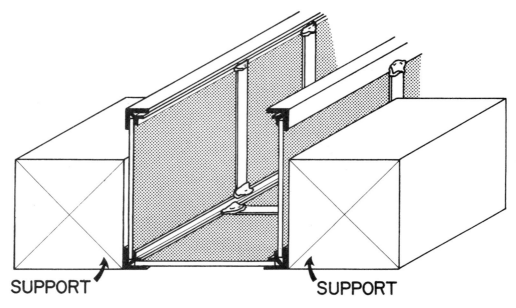

SUPPORT   SUPPORT

Figure 5-4. Attaching sides #2 and #3.

Applying the Rims

Measure and cut additional pieces of right-angle lead for the top rim of the lamp chimney. Cut the ends of the lead at a 45° angle so the joint will be a mitre joint. Use a heavy knife or hack saw. When these are cut and fitted, stand the chimney on its end and place the four pieces around the rim of the chimney and solder them to each other and also to the right-angle lead which serves as the four verticals of the chimney. (Figure 5-5.)

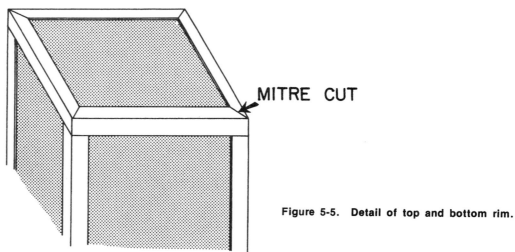

MITRE CUT

Figure 5-5. Detail of top and bottom rim.

Turn the chimney over and repeat this procedure for the bottom.

28

Touching Up The Solder Joints

If the solder joints are rough or if you wish to blend them in so that they will be more like the color of the lead, use a very stiff scrub brush to brush the entire metalwork on the shade. The scrub brush will cause the solder to take on a grayish color, and will also cause the lead to lighten somewhat.

Summary

A candle chimney is the very simplest form of lampshade, and many design possibilities exist for a wide range of expression. Shapes other than the one in this chapter can also be utilized for attractive projects.

CHAPTER 6

A STAINED GLASS LANTERN

Figure 6-1. A simple leaded glass lantern.

Stained glass lanterns can take many different shapes. They can be cylindrical, square, tapered cylinders, or combinations of these.

The one we have chosen is one of the very simplest.

All of the glass for the lantern can be cut ahead of time. The dimensions can be based on a full scale drawing. The one in our illustration has panels, 4" x 8". This can vary to suit. The design may also change to suit the location and the taste of the craftsman.

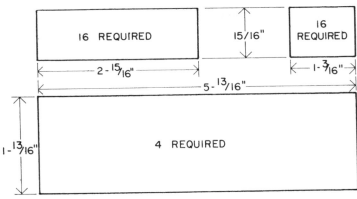

Figure 6-2. Dimensions and quantities of glass required for our leaded glass lantern.

Materials

If available, opalescent glass is the preferable type of glass to use in a lantern. For ease of assembly and neatness of final appearance we recommend a 1/4" "H" came lead. Note that the 1/4" dimension is across the face of the lead and is not the width of the channel. The width of the channel is usually standard in most lead cames and is just adequate enough to accommodate the various thicknesses of glass.

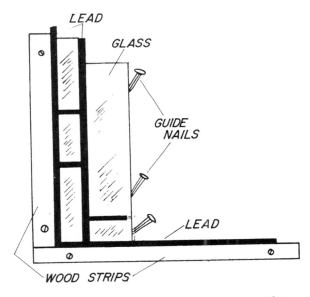

Figure 6-3. Laying out the work and starting to assemble it.

We begin by nailing two wood strips to the work table at right angles to each other. These two strips should be slightly longer than the sides of the lantern that we are trying to construct.

Cut one piece of lead channel to go along each side of the wood strip you have nailed to the workbench, and make these lead channels an inch or two longer than the length needed for the top and the side of the panels. These pieces will be trimmed off later, but at this point you do not know the exact dimension of the side or the top of the panel.

Starting in the very corner where the two leads intersect, insert the first small piece of glass into both of the channels. Cut a small piece of lead came to go along the top edge of the piece of glass so that it is slightly shorter than the glass (to allow for the vertical lead which will be added soon).

Add glass and lead alternately along your first vertical row.

As you progress, hold the glass and the lead in position on the work table with small nails.

31

After the first row of glass is put in, measure and cut a vertical lead to go along the right hand side of this row of glass. Be sure to allow a sufficient space at the top end so that the lead running along the top panel has room to fit over the glass.

Repeat these steps until all of the glass for this panel has been used.

Measure and cut the lead for the right hand edge of the panel and for the top edge of the panel and put them into place.

Apply the flux, and heat up the soldering iron and solder every place where the two pieces of lead intersect. Remove the guide nails, trim off the extra lead from the first two pieces which were installed longer than required, turn the panel over and solder it on the reverse side.

At this point, you will be able to take measurements of all of the lead came on this first panel, and use these measurements to cut all of the remaining lead for the remaining three panels. This will save time and insure uniformity in the appearance of the panel.

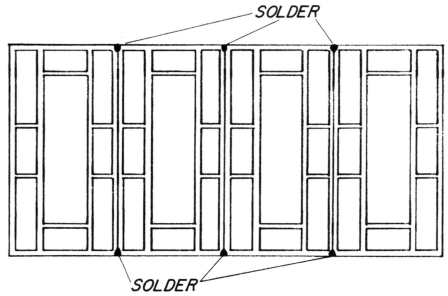

Figure 6-4. Attaching the four panels together.

Assembling the Panels

To connect the four panels together, place them side by side on the work table with all of the long edges touching. Solder every panel to the next panel near the top and near the bottom edges. This solder joint should be sufficient to hold the panel together, but not overdone. DO NOT solder the reverse sides.

Pick up the entire group of panels and place them on their edge, and gently bend at the places where the panels are joined together. The bending should be toward the side that has just been soldered. The aim is to bend the panels so that they take on the box shape of the lantern.

When the first and the last panels can be brought together, they should be soldered from the inside in the same way that the other panels are soldered together.

Cut four more pieces of lead channeling slightly longer than the length of the lantern. Twist them to form a spiral. The amount of twist is a matter of taste. Trim the length of these four pieces to suit. These pieces will fill the recess at the four corners of the lantern. Apply flux and solder them to the corners. The amount of soldering needed to accomplish this should be minimal, and you should attempt to make it as inobtrusive as possible.

Figure 6-5. Forming the box.

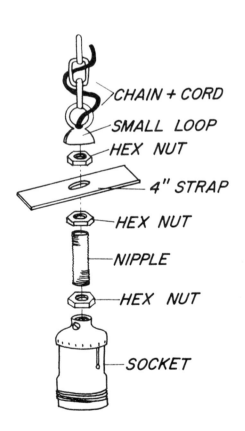

Figure 6-6. Details of the electrical work.

The installation of the electrical and hanging hardware is shown in Figure 6-6. In this instance, it is necessary to solder a steel fixture strap to the lead. It is quite difficult to solder the lead using oleic acid as a flux. It is almost necessary to use so-called "Tinners' Fluid" (available at most hardware stores) which is a diluted form of hydrofluoric acid called muriatic acid. The fixture strap must be sandpapered or cleaned with steel wool before applying the flux. A very hot iron must be used, and the steel itself must be heated to a considerable degree to make the solder adhere to it. A few experiments with the steel before attempting to solder it to the lead would be in order. Sometimes it helps to coat the steel with solder before attempting to attach it to the lead came.

33

Summary

Many interesting effects can be obtained quite simply by making four, six or even more flat leaded panels and attaching them together in a series to form a lantern.

Figure 6-7. Another interesting lantern from the turn of the century.

Figure 6-8. This lantern is more than 60 years old.

Figure 6-9. Another lantern design.

CHAPTER 7

A PANEL SHADE FOR A READING LAMP

Figure 7-1. Careful consideration in the choice of glass can enhance the appearance of any lampshade. [Photograph courtesy of Henry Marshman.]

The problem of making a lampshade in a globular or similar shape without a form upon which to build it can be approached by attempting to build portions of the lampshade on a flat surface, and when the portion has been completed, bending the entire assembly to form the shape required.

In order to attempt anything of this nature, it is almost mandatory to use lead came because the came is flexible enough to allow the manipulation required to achieve the results. By the same token, the design must be kept very simple because the very flexibility of the lead came demands simple construction so that the shape of the lampshade will contribute towards structural strength.

Where the lead came work will not be cemented, it is even more important that the structural design of the lampshade be adequate.

35

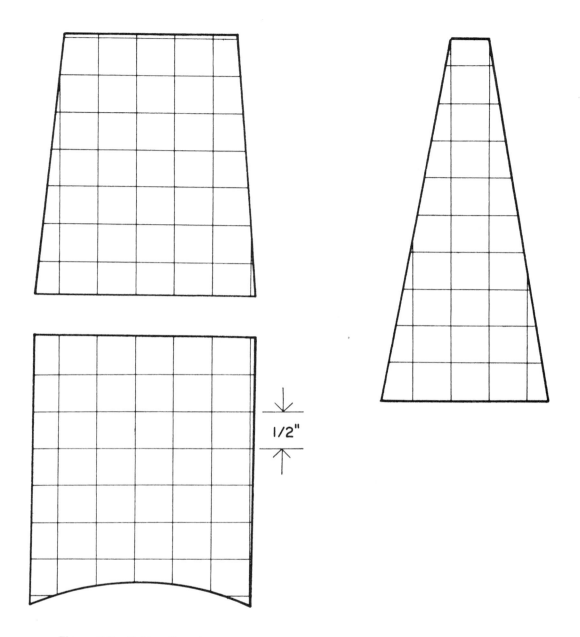

1/2"

Figure 7-2. Grid pattern lay-out. 16 pieces of each of the patterns are required.

Each block in the grid illustrated is one-half inch by one-half inch square. You may enlarge the pattern for the lampshade shown in this chapter by drawing your own grid on heavy brown paper, making the squares 1/2" x 1/2", and then copying the design as shown onto the grid. If you wish to develop your own pattern, you may do it in the same way, but you must be careful that you understand fully the consequences of altering the design. If any of the pieces taper to any greater degree than the pattern shown, the resulting lampshade will have a much flatter upper portion, and a smaller aperture.

36

Conversely, if the taper is reduced, the slope of the shade will become steeper and the aperture will become larger. Other changes can be made by adding or subtracting panels. The best way to experiment in a lampshade such as this is to lay out one pattern and make a number of copies so that you can make a cardboard or heavy paper mock-up.

We would suggest that you attempt the lampshade shown in this chapter exactly as it is designed. After making the three pattern pieces as shown, they should be cut out of the heavy paper to make them into stencils. By cutting around the stencil, or by placing the stencil beneath the glass, 16 identical glass pieces should be cut for each of the three pattern stencils.

The glass for this lampshade may be opalescent glass or cathedral glass of dark shades. The colors can be alternated or the three tiers can be made of three contrasting colors, or other color schemes may be used.

The lead came used in this lampshade should be a heavy "H" shaped lead with at least 1/4" face, except for the bottom edge, which should be a "U" shaped lead with each leg 1/8" long.

Construction Technique

The lampshade requires a work space 30" by at least 48".

Figure 7-3. Beginning of lay-out. Be sure to begin in a position that will allow the circle to be completed without going off the edge of the work board.

Figure 7-4. All work must be done with accuracy so there will be no gaps between the lead.

A length of "H" shaped lead should be laid on the workboard and curved to form the outer rim of the top tier of the shade. Using nails driven into the workboard as guides, the glass and the lead should be held in position at all times as the work progresses. Push one of the pieces of glass which forms the upper tier of the lampshade into position in the groove of the lead as shown. Hold it in place with nails as guides.

Using a scissors or a knife, cut a piece of double-channel lead for the long edge of the glass. This double channel lead should not be as long as the glass. It should be slightly shorter to make an allowance for the horizontal leads forming the bottom and top rims of this tier.

Add the next piece of glass, fitting it into the groove at the top and on the side.

Figure 7-5. It is important to place each piece into position and tap with the handle of the hammer to help straighten out the lead.

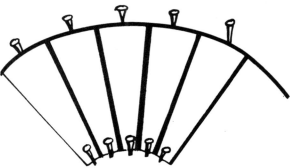

Figure 7-6. If the glass is cut accurately, there will be no difficulty in producing a perfect alignment.

Continue repeating these steps until all of the glass pieces for the top tier of the lampshade have been used. The last piece of glass installed in this fashion will have one exposed edge, which will later fit into the corresponding piece of lead which was first put down on the workboard.

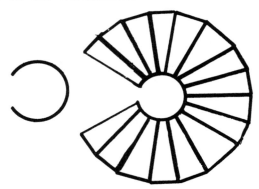

Figure 7-7. Inserting the inner ring.

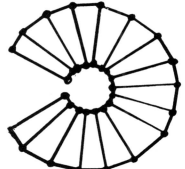

Figure 7-8. Use the minimum amount of solder required to attach the leads together.

At this point, the entire lead and glass assembly should be held in place with nails.

Cut a short piece of double-channel lead to fit around the inner circle of glass which was left exposed. Apply it to the glass, being careful that the glass is seated into the channel in all places. Use nails to hold it in position.

Soldering the Upper Tier

Scrape the areas which are going to be soldered. This may be done with the back of your scissors blade or with steel wool. These places which will be soldered will be at the intersections wherever two pieces of lead come together. The solder will cover approximately 1/4" on either side of this joint. Apply the flux and proceed with soldering all of the joints, being careful that the iron is not hot enough to melt the lead but just hot enough to melt the solder. You will note that if some of the lead cames do not fit together snugly, the solder can be "jumped" over the gap, thus filling it in.

Turn the completed section over and repeat the soldering steps on the other sides.

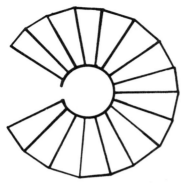

Figure 7-10. The upper portion completed.

Figure 7-9. Additional help may be required to perform the lifting and bending operation.

Forming the Upper Tier

With the smooth side of the glass up, insert your fingers into the center opening of the glass assembly and lift, thereby bringing together the two unattached edges of the glass. This should be done in gradual stages, and the bending operation should take place throughout the entire circumference of the assembly, so that each joint is bent to the same approximate degree. This action will bring the exposed edge of the last piece of glass into position to slide into the groove of the first short piece of lead which was put onto your workboard. When this connection can be made, solder the joints in the same way the other solder joints were made. Put the upper tier of the lampshade to one side.

Repeat all of the above steps on the middle section of the lampshade. The middle section, of course, has a somewhat different shape, but the method of constructing is identical.

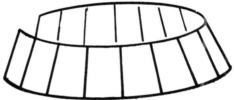

Figure 7-11. The middle section of the lampshade under construction.

Figure 7-12. Beginning the skirt.

Figure 7-13. Development of the skirt.

Assembling the Skirt Section

To assemble the skirt section, repeat the construction operation you have already used in the middle section of the lampshade. You will note that the skirt section does not curve, and therefore you may use a thin wooden strip rather than nails. The wooden strip is much more convenient, and in addition it permits a much straighter line, thus adding to the neatness of the work.

After the upper edge lead is run the full length of the skirt, and the short pieces of lead and glass are put into position, use the lead with the single channel to form the scalloped edge of the skirt.

You can use a clothes pin or the handle of a wooden tool to roll the lead to make it take the contour of the curved glass.

Figure 7-14. Approximately 48" of work space is required to completely lay out the skirt section. [Photograph courtesy of Henry Marshman.]

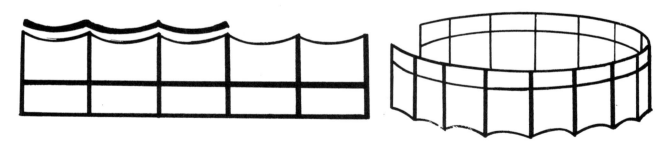

Figure 7-15. Adding the scalloped edge.

Figure 7-16. Bringing the skirt together.

Solder all the joints as before, and turn the skirt section over and repeat the soldering operation on the other side.

40

Place the skirt section onto its vertical edge and curve it so the two ends can be joined and soldered.

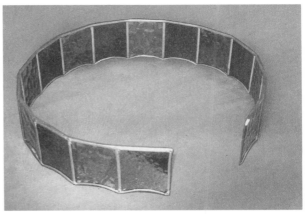

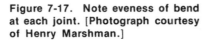

Figure 7-17. Note eveness of bend at each joint. [Photograph courtesy of Henry Marshman.]

Figure 7-18. Assembling the three separate sections.

Joining the Sections of the Lampshade

Place the middle section of the lampshade on the table and lift the upper section onto it. Seat one of the legs from the exposed lead channel from the upper section into the channel on the lower section. This may require some stretching of the lead and some bending of the two assemblies to achieve. When you have two opposite points on the lampshade seated into the channel, turn the assembly over and solder at these two points opposite each other, first making sure that the vertical leads line up. This solder joint should be no larger than is necessary to connect the upper and lower sections of the shade. The solder should be applied as closely to the existing solder as possible so that no new solder areas are created.

41

Now attempt to seat the two sections of the lampshade together in the two points furthest away from the two points already soldered. This would be at the quarter-points.

Continue to solder the two sections of the lampshade together in this fashion, gradually working from one side of the lampshade to the other in a gradual way in case the two sections of the lampshade do not exactly match. In this way, you will be stretching one of the sections just enough to accomplish the desired results.

Do not solder any of the outside joints. Do not make any of the soldering operation a continuous bead. The solder should only be applied on the inside of the shade at the areas where the vertical leads occur.

Figure 7-19. A plastic vegetable bin is a handy support for the shade while the inside is being completely soldered.

Adding the Skirt Section

To add the skirt section, the preceeding steps should be followed exactly.

When the skirt section has been added completely, the lampshade is finished as far as soldering is concerned. At this point, the lampshade can be cleaned using hot water and a dishwashing detergent to remove all traces of flux, etc. before they have a chance to harden. Be sure to dry the lampshade completely, however because any water left on will spot the lead.

Installing the Electrical and Hanging-type Hardware

The hardware shown would be the recommended type for this lampshade. The procedure for the attachment of the hardware is self-explanatory. Be sure that the upper and lower vase caps are perfectly centered onto the shade before the hex nut and ring are tightened up. If this is not done, the lampshade will not hang level.

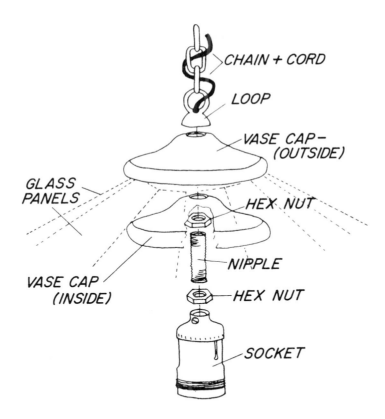

CHAIN + CORD

LOOP

VASE CAP –
(OUTSIDE)

GLASS
PANELS

HEX NUT

VASE CAP
(INSIDE)

NIPPLE

HEX NUT

SOCKET

Figure 7-20. Electrical and hanging hardware
components suggested for this lampshade.

Conclusion

There are varying degrees of complexities and varieties of lampshades which can be built in this manner. This particular type of lampshade lends itself to mass production methods, and therefore it would be best to add your own distinguishing characteristics to the design if you intend to make a lampshade such as this for your own use. There are several ways in which this may be done, such as subdividing the pattern so that some of the pieces have additional divisions in them either vertically or horizontally, or by adding overlays of metal or jewels onto the shade, or by applying distinctive electrical or hanging hardware.

43

CHAPTER 8

A HANGING CYLINDER LAMP

Figure 8-1

The technique in making a lampshade in the shape of a cylinder is somewhat different from any other, that is why we have included a chapter specifically about it. Cylinder lamps are attractive in certain situations and under certain circumstances. They usually call for a very low wattage bulb, and are used as an accessory lamp rather than as a feature.

They are suitable for porches, patios, and stair landings. They are also useful in restaurants and lounges when used singly and in groups.

44

Making the Cylinder Lamp

The top and the bottom of the lamp can be made in much the same manner.

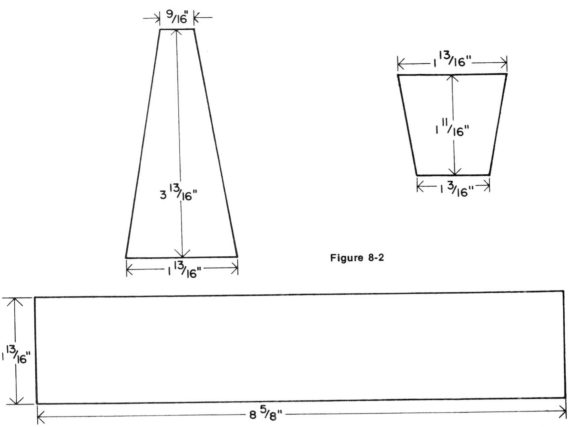

Figure 8-2

We have included a pattern of three pieces of the lampshade, giving the linear dimensions of each of the pieces. There are no curved cuts, and therefore the pattern can be given in this way rather than on a grid. Sixteen pieces of glass should be cut for each one of the three patterns. The glass may be all one color, or alternate colors of one, two, or as many as four different colors. The lead to be used in this lampshade is 1/4" "H" lead. The 1/4" dimension should be the dimension across the face. You will also need a few feet of 1/8" "U" lead. The 1/8" dimension would be the length of the leg. The work board required for this project should be at least 30" x 48".

Making the Lampshade

Using one of the double channel leads, form a portion of a curve on the work board and hold the lead in position with nails as shown. Using other nails driven into the workboard as guides, begin inserting the glass and lead together in the same way that you did in making the panel shades. You

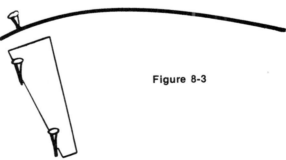

Figure 8-3

will notice that the diameter of the lampshade we are constructing in this chapter is much smaller than the panel shade and therefore the circular assembly will be much smaller.

45

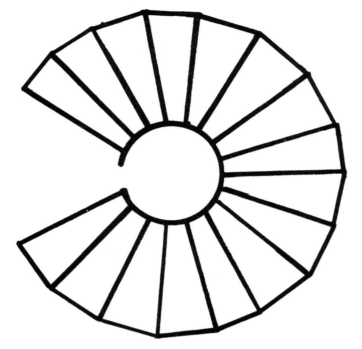

Figure 8-4

Follow the steps you used in the previous chapter on the panel lamp to construct the top and the bottom of this lampshade. The usual practice is to have the rough side of the glass facing inward.

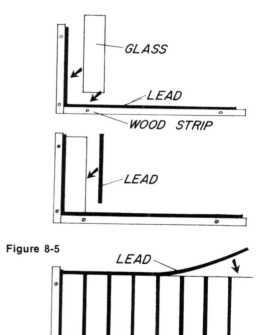

Figure 8-5

Assembling the Center Section

To assemble the center section, lay a wooden strip or lath at least 3 feet long along the bench and nail it into place. Lay another piece of lath at right angles to the first one, at least 16" long and nail it into place. Lay one of the double channel leads along the side of the long wooden strip as shown. Lay a short piece of lead along the short wooden strip as shown. The short piece of lead should be cut slightly shorter than needed to cover the edge of the glass. This allowance provides for the second long piece of lead which will be added later. Cut short pieces of lead and alternate them with the glass, until all of the glass has been used. Use guide nails to hold the assembly together as you progress. Remove the nails from along the top of the row of glass so that you may put the second long piece of lead into place. As you put it into place, replace the guide nails to hold the entire assembly together snugly.

Apply flux and solder the assembly. Turn it over and repeat the soldering operation on the other side.

46

Stand the entire assembly on its edge and curve it gently and gradually, applying pressure to the intersections between the glass so that each one takes on a slight bend, rather than trying to accomplish the entire bending operation at one portion of the assembly. You may have to apply the pressure around the perimeter of the assembly several times before you get the desired amount of bend.

When you have curved the entire assembly into the proper shape, the last piece of glass will slip into the open channel of the first piece of lead, and you then may solder it on the outside as well as on the inside.

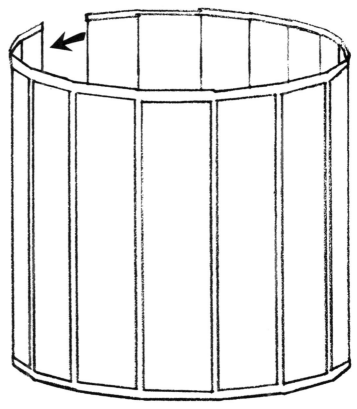

Figure 8-6

Joining the Sections

Place the lower section of the lampshade onto the table. Lift the center section onto it. Join these two sections in the same way that you joined the sections of the panel lamp earlier.

After you have completely soldered these two sections together, place the upper part of the lampshade on the workbench and turn the two assembled pieces over and join them to this upper portion.

Clean the lampshade in the same way the panel shade in the previous chapter was cleaned.

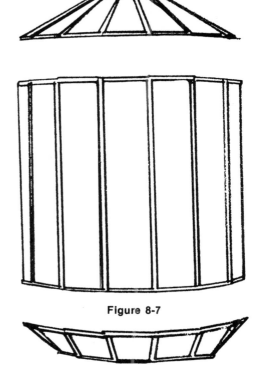

Figure 8-7

Electrical and Hanging Hardware

For your convenience we have repeated the sketch of the electrical and hanging hardware used on the other lampshade. This electrical and hanging hardware group is quite standard in lamps of this type. Portions of it can be bought at electrical supply stores or hardware stores, and the entire assembly is also offered as a complete package by certain craft dealers or stained glass supply houses.

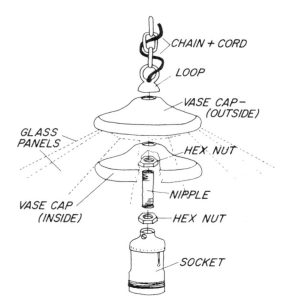

CHAIN + CORD

LOOP

VASE CAP— (OUTSIDE)

GLASS PANELS

HEX NUT

NIPPLE

VASE CAP (INSIDE)

HEX NUT

SOCKET

Figure 8-8

Variations of This Design

This design admits of many, many variations which are limited only by the imagination. The large expanse of center panels fairly cry out for subdividing in some way. Scrap glass, remnants, and unusable pieces of very small dimension can be combined into these side panels. The narrowness of the strip allows the use of many small pieces of glass and the design can be simply stacks of glass cut into strips, or it can be made of random angles. The entire area encompassed by the long strip of glass in the lampshade is free to experiment with, as long as the vertical lead strips are left undisturbed.

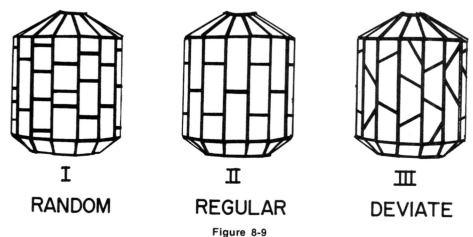

I
RANDOM

II
REGULAR

III
DEVIATE

Figure 8-9

Another variation that can be used in this lampshade is to lengthen or shorten the strips.

Summary

The cylindrical lampshade is one of the most versatile patterns for a small lampshade, and is very encouraging to the amateur because of its ease of assembly and latitude of design possibilities.

CHAPTER 9

MAKING A STAINED GLASS LAMPSHADE DOME USING LEAD CAME

The making of a leaded glass shade using came involves some special consideration as to the design. Lead came is very pliable and therefore when designing the shade, some thought should be given to the structural strength of the finished product. The lampshade shown in our illustration is dependent upon the continuous tiers of glass and lead which form an arch around the entire body of the shade. If these were not straight lines, considerable stresses and strains would develop and the lampshade would be a problem to construct and keep in shape.

Figure 9-1. This lampshade uses lead cames for the metalwork.

Further strength is achieved by the cementing process which introduces a material between the lead and the glass containing plaster-of-Paris or portland cement, which eventually hardens to a very stiff consistancy and "sets" the lampshade into a permanent shape. In addition, certain places may need reinforcement with copper wires which can be applied on the inside of the shade.

Patterns

After selecting a form or, if necessary, constructing a form, the pattern must be developed. In our lampshade, we have shown a skirt approximately 4" deep. In order to design the segment of the pattern for the skirt it is necessary to cut a wide strip of heavy paper long enough to go around the entire circumference of the lampshade. As soon as you have begun this part of the process you will immediately perceive that the paper pattern will not lie flat against the form because the form is curved on two planes. What you actually need here, then, is to make a paper strip which will be a segment of a cone whose apex is some distance above the sphere (depending upon the angle of the segment to the perpendicular axis of the sphere). In other words, depending upon the amount of inward lean to the skirt section, your skirt pattern when flattened out will be either a straight pattern or a curved pattern. Our skirt has an inward lean to it so we therefore have a slightly curved skirt section. (See Figure 9—2.) Once you have a usable segment of pattern for the skirt, you may continue similarly up the form, laying out strips for each tier. This preliminary work is entirely mechanical and mathematical, and the actual

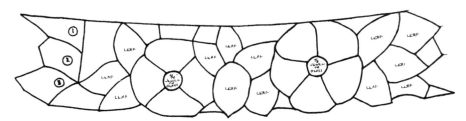

Figure 9-2. This is the complete pattern for one-fourth of the skirt. Note how the end pieces interlock with the adjacent pieces from the next section. This lampshade pattern was developed for a 22" diameter shade form.

designing of the pattern can wait until later. Due to the amount of time and effort which will go into the glass cutting and soldering later on, it would be almost advisable to tape the entire pattern layouts together to be doubly sure that they are the right shape before you proceed any further with the patterning.

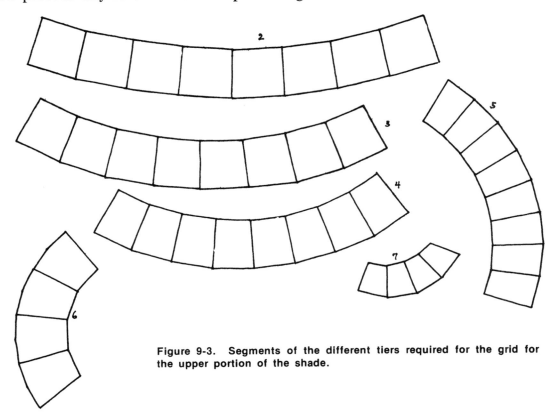

Figure 9-3. Segments of the different tiers required for the grid for the upper portion of the shade.

Once your arithmetic is correct, you may flatten out the patterns, and depending upon your ultimate design of the lampshade, you should now consider how many repeats there should be in the design.

It is obvious that to the eye, only slightly less than 50% of the lampshade can be seen at any one time. It is desirable, then, in most instances to have repeats in the design. This allows for the viewer to see the entire pattern or design from any side of the shade and also helps somewhat in the making of the shade. In any event, if the upper parts of the lampshade are to be a grid work consisting of trapezoidal shapes, the only portion we are concerned about is the skirt. If the skirt is to have repeats in it, you should divide the skirt into equal sections of two, three or four equal parts, and create

50

your design upon the paper. You will note that the lower edge of the skirt need not be straight, but can be irregular if desired. The upper edge of the skirt must be straight in order to meet with the first tier of the grid-work above.

Make your pattern definite and legible, because you will need to make additional copies.

Using additional heavy paper, make two carbon copies of one section of the skirt. If you are having three repeats, for instance, this means that you should make two additional copies of one-third of the skirt pattern. One of these copies is to be cut up into stencils, and the other copy is the one to stack the cut pieces of glass on for reference purposes. Your original skirt pattern (which is the complete length of the skirt) is your working paper upon which you will assemble the glass and lead.

Before taking the drawings apart and removing the carbon papers, go over the portion of the skirt that has been drawn in triplicate and number every piece beginning with Number One. In addition, go over the entire portion of the drawings that is reproduced in triplicate and put a color code on every piece of glass. The reason for numbering and color coding the pieces is that once the pieces have been cut apart and made into stencils it is surprising how similar they are. It would be easy to get them mixed and spend much time later in sorting them out.

At this point, you should have one complete drawing of the skirt plus two copies consisting of only a portion of the skirt (depending upon how many repeats you have elected).

Cutting Out the Stencils

It is apparent that at this point some provision has to be made for the fact that the lead came which will be used in the making of this shade will occupy some of the space depicted on the drawing. In order to eliminate a space wide enough to accommodate the web of the lead came, it is necessary to cut out the stencils slightly smaller than they appear on the drawing.

For many years stained glass craftsmen have used various tools for this purpose. There are double-bladed pattern shears which eliminate a thin strip of paper when they are used to cut out stencils. A similar tool is called a double-bladed pattern knife. For our purposes, we can take two single-edged razor blades and sandwich a thin piece of cardboard (approximately 1/16th") between them and tape this sandwich together or wrap rubber bands

Figure 9-4. Double-bladed pattern shears made especially for producing stencils with allowances for the heart of the lead came.

51

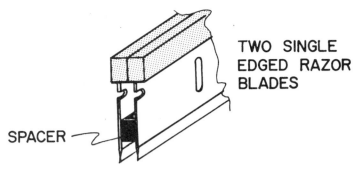

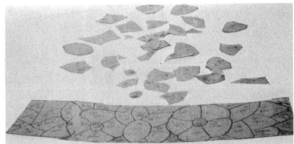

TWO SINGLE
EDGED RAZOR
BLADES

SPACER

Figure 9-5. An inexpensive substitute for double-bladed pattern shears.

Figure 9-6. Stencils and working drawing.

around it. Taking the second copy of your pattern (the first carbon copy, that is) you may now proceed to cut out every piece of the pattern. Henceforth, these separate pieces will be refered to as "stencils". Each stencil will be 1/32nd" smaller all around than its corresponding piece on the pattern.

At this juncture you should have a numbered, intact working drawing consisting of a portion of the skirt of the lampshade, plus a set of numbered stencils corresponding with this numbered working drawing, plus a pattern of the entire skirt.

Figure 9-7. Cutting the glass from the stencils.

Cutting the Glass

After sorting the stencils by color, begin cutting the glass. You will note that more than one piece of glass must be cut for each stencil if your pattern is a repeating pattern. If your pattern repeats three times, for instance, you must make three pieces first so that the smaller pieces can be cut from scraps.

Take particular care to position the grain of the variegations in the opal glass to follow the natural lines of the leaves or arrange the grain to simulate the veins in any of the floral portions of the design.

In an earlier chapter we discussed various ways of handling stencils when cutting glass to pattern. It will soon be obvious that in this instance the stencils must be laid on top of the glass and the glass cutter used in the manner of a scribing tool to cut around the edge of the stencil, being careful to keep the wheel against the edge of the stencil so that the piece of glass cut will not be larger than the stencil. As you cut the glass, stack the identical pieces of glass one on top of the other and place them in a group upon the last copy of the pattern. If you have two or three pieces of the same number, put the stencil piece between the top two pieces to keep it from being blown away. This will serve as a check against your cutting procedure to make sure that you do not recut glass needlessly.

Glazing the Skirt

We have selected "U" shaped lead with 1/8" legs for the bottom edge of the skirt. We will use "H" lead with a 3/16" face for the top edge of the skirt. The rest of the lead came will be "H" lead with a 1/8" face.

Begin glazing at the left side of the skirt working drawing and work to the right. Use plenty of nails driven into the workboard to hold the left hand pieces of the skirt in position on the workboard, because they will take quite a bit of pounding as you tap subsequent pieces into position.

Figure 9-8. Glazing the skirt.

The "H" shaped lead came which forms the upper border of the skirt should be put into position at the very beginning and left its full length. This means that if your lampshade is 20" in diameter, you will be working on a skirt which will eventually be between 60 and 70 inches long, and therefore you must begin at the far end of your workbench and use your complete skirt drawing as a working drawing. This double-channel lead will therefore need to stretch the full length, and have a back-up of nails at frequent intervals as a fence to insure that it follows the skirt drawing. Don't be afraid of using too many nails.

The "U" shaped lead which will form the bottom edge of the skirt should be allowed to remain its full length also. The nails to hold it in place will have to be added as you proceed with the glazing, otherwise you will create situations in which you will be unable to insert the glass at certain stages of the operation.

The intermediate lead (consisting of the smallest "H" shaped round lead you can obtain) should be used in as long pieces as possible consistant with workability. Only experience can guide you as to the direction to take. Certainly, the lead around jewels and other pre-formed pieces should be made of all one piece of lead.

The glass will have to be tapped with the end of your hammer to make sure it seats into the lead as far as possible as it is exactly over the pattern line. As you work along, you must make certain that both of these conditions are being met, or you will have to recut some glass to achieve this condition. Any places where you can see a space between the glass and the lead will only get worse when the skirt is bent.

When you have reached the end of the working drawing, apply your flux, and solder all the joints. Do not solder the reverse side of the skirt. With only one side soldered, you will be able to bend it much easier.

When you have completely soldered the entire skirt to your own satisfaction, stand the finished portion of the work upon its lower edge. You may need help with this procedure, if help is available.

Figure 9-9. Putting the skirt onto the form. Note that it is unnecessary to drive nails or pins into the form to hold the work in place when working with lead came.

Place the form against something immovable, and place the center of the bottom edge of the skirt section you have made onto the table and against the bottom of the form and gently begin to bend the entire skirt. It is quite possible to break glass if this is not done carefully. It should be a gradual process, and be done in easy stages from one end of the section to the other. Keep the gradual bending operation going until the entire skirt is wrapped around the form and it is as snug as possible. It may be difficult to maintain this snugness at all points and at all times due to a lack of enough hands. A stout cord assisted by a heavy rubber band to make a sort of girdle is helpful in this operation.

Do not be alarmed if there is a distance between your leaded glass skirt and the form. As much as 1/4" would be there if you put the paper pattern onto the form because the contact between the skirt and the form occurs 2" from the bottom of the form. The upper edge of the skirt should also be a slight distance away from the form.

It would be almost impossible to get to this point and not have to cut a few pieces of glass over again, and not have to rearrange some lead, etc. This is quite a task because of the angles and number of spots which need to be joined. Once you have joined a couple of places, however, you can make paper patterns for the special pieces of glass and keep testing them until you have just what you need. These final few pieces are difficult and important.

B. The Body

The first tier of glass to make up the body of the illustrated shade will be handled differently than that of the skirt.

Prepare two copies of the pattern, using heavy brown paper as before.

Use one copy as your working drawing. Rather than cutting out multiple stencils, cut out just one, using the stencil scissors or a double-bladed razor blade.

Next, construct a simple jig with which you can cut the strip of the glass you intend to use for the body of the shade. (See Figure 9-10.) Cut several strips, and from these strips cut several pieces to the pattern of the stencil you have made. By alternately reversing the top and the bottom of the stencil, you will find that you will only have to make one cut each time you cut a piece from the 2" strip. Cut enough short pieces of the small "H" channel lead to glaze one section. In cutting these short pieces, be sure to allow for the bottom and top horizontal leads.

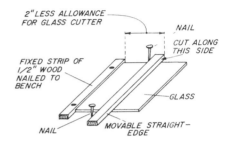

Figure 9-10. Simple jig for cutting a grid pattern.

Figure 9-11 shows how this section should be glazed. You will note that there is no bottom lead which makes for some difficulty when it is time to pick the whole thing up to put into place. You might want to try glazing it with the smooth side down, and running a length of masking tape across it.

Figure 9-11. Glazing the second tier. [The first grid tier.]

In any event, you must now get the section of pieces onto the form, and guide all the pieces of glass tightly into the bottom lead. You may want to do your soldering before you have leaned this glass inward to contact the form. If this is done, the glass will tend to seat itself more firmly into the lead. (Figure 9-12.)

Figure 9-12. Placing the second tier onto the skirt.

Once the soldering is done on this section, check the mathematics of the work. If this section is supposed to equal one-fourth of the circumference of the form, and it does not total this amount, you should make adjustments on the succeeding sections. Try to avoid making any piece more than 1/8th" different in width from an adjacent piece.

As you work around this row of glass, check and recheck your work. Be sure the glass is contacting the form. This will insure a symmetrical result.

The last two pieces of glass in this row will have to be cut especially to fit the remaining space allotted to them. We suggest making paper patterns. These two pieces will be installed at the same time and will have to be tapped into place with the handle of your hammer.

The remaining rows of glass in this shade will require a different treatment because you will want your vertical lead cames to line up with the ones below.

No matter how careful you are, it is almost impossible to cut another row of eight pieces from pattern row #3 and install it onto the shade form in such a way that all of the vertical leads line up. The reason for this is that if you have made any of your pieces even 1/16" too large or too small the accumulation of several such errors can result in things not lining up as much as 1/4".

Installing this tier on top of tier #2 will only compound such errors.

The procedure henceforth should be as follows:

Prepare another paper stencil for one piece of glass as you did for the previous tier. Cut several pieces of glass to this stencil. Stand them in the groove of the top lead on tier #2, and let them lean against the form. When they are leaning against the form, the adjacent edges of each piece

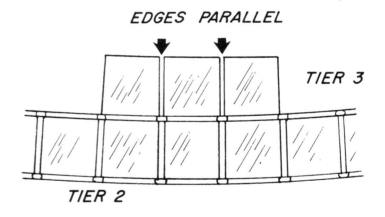

Figure 9-13. Checking the accuracy of the glass cutting for the third tier.

should be exactly parallel, and show an even space between them. (See Figure 9—13.) If this does not occur, adjust your pattern until it does.

Once this condition is met you should prepare two pieces of glass and three short leads as shown in figure 9—14. It will be necessary to drive nails to hold this arrangement in place while soldering. After soldering, transfer this group to the shade, and solder in place, first making sure that the vertical leads line up.

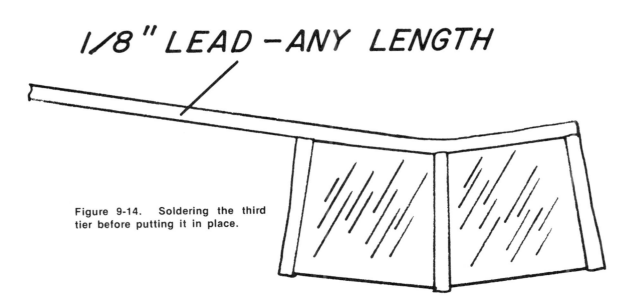

1/8" LEAD - ANY LENGTH

Figure 9-14. Soldering the third tier before putting it in place.

Now take your paper stencil and hold it in the place where the next piece of glass to the left will go. If a piece of glass cut to this stencil will be the correct size, and allow the next lead vertical to line up, cut a piece of glass and install it and solder another short piece of lead into place.

If the paper stencil discloses that the next piece should be larger or smaller, you should cut a piece to suit. In this way, you will insure that all your verticals will line up.

You will not need to check the mathematics on this tier, because you are following the row below, and it is correct. You will have to install the last two pieces in this row the same way you did for row #2.

Proceed with the next 2 rows in exactly the same manner as this row.

The next row up is slightly different in that there is a "V" shape at the bottom of each piece of glass to conform to the angle made by the two pieces of glass in the row below it. (See Figure 9-15.)

In actuality, however, due to the fact that the top lead on the next tier down doesn't make this sharp angle, but rather makes a curve, you will have to adjust your paper stencil for this condition also. You will find that hardly any of these pieces will be identical, so many adjustments will have to be made. Other than this, this row will also need to be checked for distance from the crown. Rather than have the hole at top off center, it might be well to begin to make any adjustments necessary in this row.

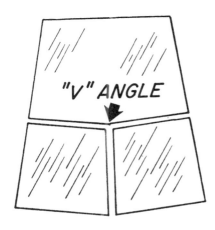

"V" ANGLE

Figure 9-15. Modification at the top tier.

57

The final row of pieces are similar to the previous row, but each piece will also have to be adjusted for height because it is necessary to leave a hole at the top no greater than 4" in diameter. The top lead, incidently, is still to be 1/8" round "H".

The shade form can be inverted and placed in a large waste basket, ash barrel or similar vessel whose inside diameter is less than 22", and whose occupants will not be needing it for a short while. (See Figure 9-16.)

Before proceeding, now is the proper time to go over the shade visually for places where the glass has popped out of the lead, or where you can see daylight between the lead and the glass. These things can be corrected in some instances by pushing the lead came one way or another.

Figure 9-16. Using a waste basket for a support.

Once this is accomplished, place the inverted shade gently into the inverted form. Apply flux, and solder the portion which can be worked in this position, then rotate the shade and repeat for the next portion.

Electrical and Hanging Equipment

At this juncture, you should install the ring, the inner crown and the outer crown. Figure 9—17 shows the relationship of these various devices to one another and to the shade. Be sure to center the upper crown so that the same amount of margin is visible on all sides of the top row of glass. This is all of the electrical and hanging equipment which should be installed at this time.

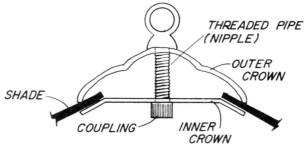

Figure 9-17. Suggested electrical and hanging hardware lay-out.

Reinforcing

At this point, depending upon the design, any reinforcing wires needed for this work should be installed.

Placing the lampshade inside the inverted form once again, reinforcing wires should be soldered in place where necessary.

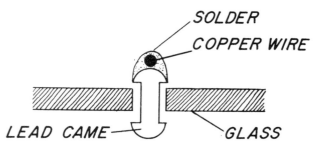

Figure 9-18. Reinforcing certain vertical leads.

58

In this particular shade, every fourth vertical came should have a copper wire soldered to it continuously on the inside of the lampshade from the upper edge of the skirt up to and including the edge of the inner crown. The inner crown, being brass, will accept solder readily. In addition to the spot where the wire joins the inner crown, the inner crown should also be soldered to every vertical came around its entire circumference. (See Figure 9—18.) This reinforcement and soldering work insures against the possibility of the lampshade sagging or any of the solder joints coming apart due to the weight of the shade.

Cementing

Cementing is the term used in leaded glass work for the grouting or filling-in of all the spaces between the glass and channels of the lead cames. This process, in the case of a window, makes it waterproof. Of equal importance, however, is the amount of stiffness and strength it adds to the finished piece.

Even after cementing, the shade will feel rather flimsy. After a few weeks, when the cement has taken a good set, the shade will become almost rigid.

The lampblack in the cement has the further effect of darkening the lead, which most people find comforting.

Furthermore, the act of cementing cleans off all the flux and gives the whole shade a high polish.

Inasmuch as leaded glass cementing is in the same league as chimney cleaning, boiler inspecting, chicken roost scraping and automobile engine rebuilding when judged by the amount of dirt and debris it scatters in all directions, act accordingly.

You will need the following material and equipment:

5#	Plaster of Paris
2#	Whiting
1 Qt.	Linseed Oil
2 Qt.	Turpentine (**not** paint thinner)
1 oz.	Lampblack
1	Painter's Pail
1	Old 2 Quart Pan
Pair	Work Gloves
2	**Stiff** bristle scrub brushes (about 8")
1	Pointed 1/4" dowel or stick
	Fine Sawdust (about a peck)
	Rags
	Stirring stick or wooden spoon

Mix half of the plaster (2½ lbs.) and half of the whiting (1 lb.) in the painters pail.

In an old pan, pour 1 quart turpentine and 1 pint linseed oil.

Add the liquid to the solids gradually, stirring them together as you add. When the mixture has reached the consistancy of a very heavy cake batter, stop adding liquids, This consistancy should be maintained throughout the cementing operation. It may be necessary to add some liquid later on. If your cement becomes too fluid, add plaster of Paris (no whiting) until it returns to the proper consistancy.

Next, add your lampblack in sufficient quantity to get a very black color throughout.

Clean everything off your bench and put down several layers of newspaper. Put the shade form on the bench, right side up, with the shade on top of it.

Using the stick or wooden spoon, transfer blobs of the cement onto the shade on the side facing you. With one of the scrub brushes, brush this cement copiously across the face of the shade in both directions, so that every square inch of the shade is covered, and every lead came has had cement forced into every crevice.

Cement the entire surface of the shade in this manner. Then proceed to remove the excess cement from the surface of the glass and face of the lead, using the brush to push the cement into piles, and to lift it off the shade. Scrape it off the brush, back into the pail.

Next, put a handful of sawdust into a rag, and rub the sawdust briskly onto the shade. Remove as much cement as you can with this procedure. When you have finished, you will still have deposits and residues of cement all around the lead cames. Leave this for now.

Figure 9-19. Cementing department in a commercial studio. Notice sawdust being applied to remove excess solder from window.

Remove the shade from the form. Wipe off any cement that has leaked through onto the form, and invert the form into the wastebasket or ash can once more. Once again, place the inverted shade into the inverted form. Cement the inside of the shade in the same manner that you cemented the outside. Then let it all set for about 2 hours.

The next operation is called "picking", and may take as long as one or 2 hours.

With your pointed stick (sharpened in a pencil sharpener) dig out, or "trim" the excess cement from around the perimeter of each piece of glass on the inside of the shade. This operation will "cut" the excess cement back to the edge of the lead came, and eliminate all but the hidden portion of the cement. With a few minutes practice, you will be able to do this quite rapidly, in one continuous motion. (Figure 9-20.)

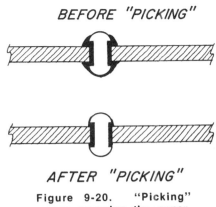

BEFORE "PICKING"

AFTER "PICKING"

Figure 9-20. "Picking" means removing the super-fluous cement.

With a rag, brush or whip the droppings out of the shade cavity as you go along, so that you will be getting rid of the excess cement once and for all.

When you have finished picking the inside of the shade, pick up a handful of clean sawdust, and with the second brush (as yet unused), brush the inside of the shade briskly and thoroughly, until every vestige of grease and cement are gone.

Wipe out the sawdust from the inside of the shade, and take another handful of sawdust and repeat the operation with a course rag. Rub and rub until the whole thing shines.

Now remove the shade from the form. Clean off any cement from the form, especially the outside. Put the form onto the bench, right side up, and place the shade upon it.

Now you can "pick" the cement from this side of the shade, and repeat every part of the procedure you just finished on the inside of the shade.

When you have finished this step, allow the shade to sit overnight on the shade form. This will allow the cement to take an initial "set" while the shade is held rigid on the form.

The Finish

Remove the shade from the form, and install the electrical items. You will observe that this is simply a matter of wiring the sockets and pulling the wire through the conduit and the ring.

After putting the chain onto the ring, find somewhere nearby to hang the shade and plug in the cord. With the lights on, inspect the silhouettes of the lead to see if any more picking needs to be done.

Check to see if any light shows through between the lead and the glass. If it does, fill some of your left-over cement into the chinks in a neat manner, and attempt to make it look as if you intended to do it that way right along.

Summary

With some modifications, the steps you have used in this chapter are the same steps you would use in making any leaded glass shade consisting of relatively large quantities of small pieces of glass. There are advantages and disadvantages using this method, and as we proceed into other types of lampshade work you will discover what these advantages and disadvantages are.

CHAPTER 10

A LARGE HANGING CONE-SHAPED LAMPSHADE USING A FORM

Figure 10-1. The completed hanging cone shade.

Heretofore we have described methods of making lampshades with lead cames in which portions of the work were done in segments on a flat surface, and then these portions were bent to take on the shape of the finished lampshade. It is obvious that such methods impose many restrictions upon the craftsman. Designs are very limited, and techniques are inhibited. It is apparent that if the lampshade can be built upon a solid shape or form, and if some other method can be found to hold the glass together which will add strength and rigidity to the finished lampshade, a large avenue of design possibilities can be opened.

These two problems are solved in this chapter.

Several possibilities exist in the creation of lampshade forms. In a simple conical shape, it is possible to construct a lampshade form out of very heavy poster board, sheet metal, heavy tagboard, or other heavy sheet material which will remain rigid and bear the weight of the glass and the metal as it is applied.

Other shapes require specialized handling. In the original studios which specialized in making lampshades in the latter part of the 19th century, permanent lampshade forms were made and used over and over again. These permanent lampshade forms were either turned on a lathe from hardwood such as maple or hard pine, or they were manufactured out of heavy sheet metal and welded into the proper shapes. These shapes may have been cones, globes, bells or combinations of shapes quite familiar to anyone who has seen illustrations of old lampshade art.

You can readily see that the expense involved in producing permanent lampshade forms which will be used only once or twice at the most puts somewhat of a restraint on the amateur.

Fortunately, there are materials today which, although they cannot be classified as permanent, do allow some degree of re-use, and even though the expense of making the form may run as much as $15 or $20, the expense is bearable if the form is to be used several times or if the lampshade being produced is ultimately to be worth several hundreds of dollars.

One of the most popular materials for use in making lampshades is Styrofoam®. Styrofoam® can be purchased in some of the larger craft stores or directly from dealers in the larger cities. It comes in block sizes which can be cemented together to produce blocks large enough from which to make lampshade forms. After the Styrofoam has been cemented together, a large kitchen knife can be used to cut and shape the form to the size desired.

Figure 10-1A. A lamp form made from Styrofoam. This particular shape is a modified globe.

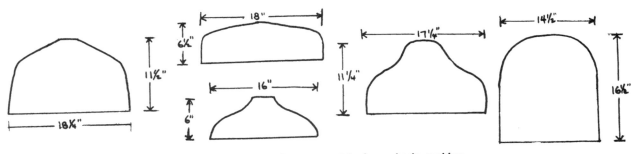

Figure 10-2. Other shapes used in lampshade making.

If you do not consider the time and effort involved to be worth it, you may purchase Styrofoam® lampshade forms already shaped. They range in cost from $8.00 to $35.00 depending upon the size. There are several sources of these lampshade forms.

Lampshade forms can also be made from papier-maché. There are other materials which can be used for this purpose, but the main consideration for the amateur is to make the shade form from a material into which nails or pins can be driven. A solid form made from a material such as sheet metal requires that the glass and metal be taped into place as you go along, and we feel that tacking or nailing the material into place is easier.

The Copper Foil Method

Presuming the problem of lampshade forms to be solved to your satisfaction, we attack the next problem, that of the metal to be used to hold the pieces of glass together.

There are obvious limitations to lead. It is pliable and soft. Even the smallest of the double-channel leads shows a sight-line of 1/8" in width. The use of lead in many small pieces requires very intricate manipulations when the work is progressing, and one may expect at times to have as many as a dozen pieces of lead being fed into the work area at one time.

These problems require little or no imagination to suggest a solution. The metal being used must be a rigid material and yet be so pliable that it will follow the contour of even the most intricately cut piece of glass. The method used since the very outset of the so-called "leaded glass lampshade" in the 19th century and the method described in an earlier chapter, is the use of foil. After the glass was cut to pattern, sheets of copper foil 1/1,000ths of an inch thick were cut into 1/4" wide or 3/16th" wide strips. An adhesive was brushed onto the foil, and the foil was wrapped around the edge of the glass. The foil was smoothed down onto the glass with the back of a teaspoon or perhaps a shoe horn so that it formed a channel in the shape of the letter "U" around the edge of every piece of glass. After all of the glass was wrapped with this foil, the pieces of glass were assembled onto the pattern upon the lampshade form, held in place with nails, pins or tape, and continuous beads of solder were applied along the joint between every piece of glass and its adjacent piece.

The solder contained anywhere from 40% to 50% lead, and therefore, as in any other soldering process, this was called "leading". The lampshade, then, was called a "leaded glass shade". Actually, however, it was a lampshade made with glass and copper foil, and the copper foil was plated with tin (the other ingredient is solder) and lead. The tin, of course, was the ingredient in the solder which gave the rigidity. When the lampshade was removed from the form, it was absolutely stiff.

The procedure was repeated on the inside of the shade on almost all cases, except in the shop of the **Price-Cutter** down the street, who sold his lampshades for $1.50 less than those of the quality shop we are talking about.

Getting Down to Business

Now that we have cleared up these two little points, you can be sure that we will have no difficulty in whipping through a 24" hanging cone shade in jig time.

Bill and Sheila Blair who operate The Glass House, in Kingston, Ontario allowed us to peek into their workrooms which are simply crawling with beautiful Canadian girls who do some almost unbelievable things with glass.

The Blairs have a very successful stained and leaded glass business, and sell custom made lampshades and other stained glass products for customers in all parts of Canada. They do their own designing, and undertake commissions for restaurants and similar installations entailing the manufacture of the complete lamps including chandeliers and supporting hardware.

The lampshade pattern used in this chapter was designed by Bill Blair.

Figure 10-3. Beginning the patterning.

The Pattern

Cut a piece of stiff paper large enough to wrap around the lamp form. Cut the two edges so that the paper is the exact size of the complete lampshade.

Divide the paper into vertical divisions representing the number of repeating sections you intend to use in the design. The more repeats you use the less designing and cartooning you will have to do. The lampshade we are seeing built in this chapter has nine repeats.

66

In this project, one method of designing is shown. It involves the use of a repeating cluster of flowers. Mr. Blair has cleverly designed the clusters so that they can be turned in different directions. You will note that it has been used this way in his design, and the areas between clusters have been adjusted and filled in so that the clusters interlock.

Continuing with the development of the drawing, each piece in the design is now numbered, and a color is written upon it. Note also that the background has been ruled off as a beginning toward incorporating the background grid pattern.

This work is being done on a flat surface.

Figure 10-4. Beginning of the development of the grid.

Repeating the design nine times on the pattern sheet completes the pattern. You will note that in this instance, only one copy of the pattern was made. In many instances it is desirable to have additional copies of the pattern. This is particularly necessary when you desire to make more than one lampshade from the same pattern, or if there are extremely large quantities of glass to be cut and it is necessary to have a pattern to lay the cut glass onto for storage where they can easily be identified, or, in instances where there are very few repeats in the

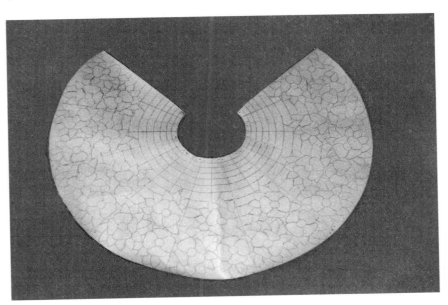

Figure 10-5. The completed basic pattern.

67

lampshade it is desirable to cut the entire pattern up for stencils, making it necessary to have an additional drawing to put onto the form as a working drawing.

In our example, only one of the nine pattern sections will be cut into stencils, and nine pieces of glass will be cut from each of these stencils.

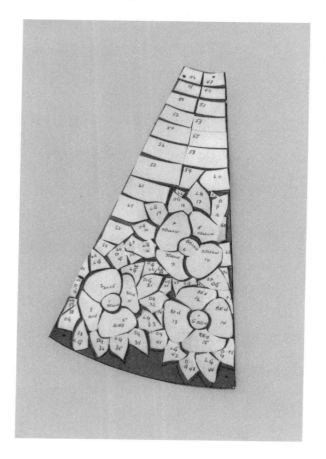

Figure 10-6. One section stencilled.   Figure 10-7. Keeping track of the pieces of glass.

Inasmuch as the stencil will be used nine times, it would be best to trace the pattern onto some tagboard or thin cardboard of the thickness of a manila folder, and to use these for your cutting. Be sure to include the piece number and the color information when you trace the pattern onto the card stock.

Assemble the stencils as shown.

Cutting the Glass

Cut nine pieces of glass for each stencil. Stack them on a copy of the pattern in groups of nine. This will help determine the progress of the cutting, and also help identify the cut pieces when you are ready to use them. Note that no allowance is made for the thickness of the metal, and the glass is cut to the full size of the pattern.

Figure 10-8. Wrapping the glass with foil.

Figure 10-9. The foil must be attached securely to the glass.

Applying the Copper Foil

Starting with the pieces which will be used at the top part of the lampshade, begin wrapping every piece of glass around its perimeter with 1/4" wide or 3/16" wide copper foil. The copper foil is obtainable through craft stores in sheets, and is also manufactured in rolls 1/4" wide or 3/16" wide with a pressure sensitive adhesive backing. This pressure sensitive variety is much easier to use, and even in production shops it is preferred because the saving in labor more than compensates for the extra cost. The copper foil should be applied to the edge of the glass so that the margin which laps onto the face of the glass on each side is equal. As the pieces are accumulated, they should be applied to the lampshade forming groups and held in place with pins, nails, or toothpicks. You will note that the complete pattern has been applied to the lampshade form and as the lampshade pieces are applied to the form, great care must be taken that the pieces are actually fitting into the spaces allotted for them. If they are not, the trifling errors which occur will only repeat themselves and accumulate into large errors which will become quite unsightly. If you do not seem to be following the pattern, you must remove the foil from some of your glass and recut it, or nip off the pieces which are required to make the glass the correct size. If your foil does not adhere to the edge of the glass properly, you may press it down and insure a tight fit by rubbing it with the back of a teaspoon, a popsickle stick, or a shoehorn.

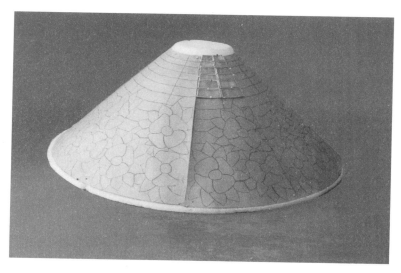

Figure 10-10. Some of the pieces in place on the form.

Figure 10-11. Adding more pieces.

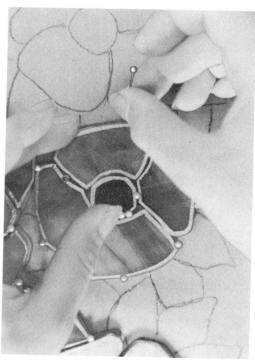

Figure 10-12. A closer detail of the pinning operation.

As you get larger and larger areas of your lampshade form covered with glass, you will see the advisibility of soldering the pieces together in occasional spots to keep the whole assembly from popping off accidently. This procedure is called "tack soldering", and you needn't be too fussy about the workmanship or technique in doing it because the solder you apply at this time will be remelted when the final soldering job is done. It is necessary, however, to provide some way of holding the glass onto the form once you

70

have several dozen pieces applied, because as you will observe, the pins or nails only surround the perimeter of the group of glass, and nothing is holding the center pieces onto the form except gravity.

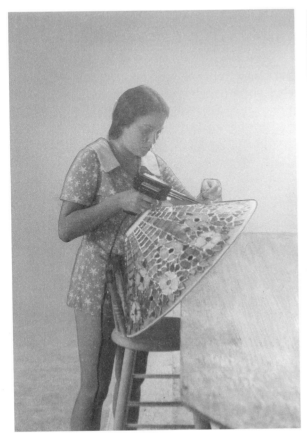

Figure 10-14. Removing the shade from the form.

Figure 10-13.   Soldering   the outside of the shade.

Figure 10-15. Soldering the inside of the lampshade.

Soldering the Lampshade

After all of the pieces of glass are cut, wrapped with foil, and tack soldered into place on the form, your soldering may begin in earnest.

The solder must be applied in even beads, and the finished line of solder should be slightly convex, and give the appearance of being a continuous piece of metal. The lampshade we are illustrating has so much soldering in it that when you build it you undoubtedly will become quite adept at this operation before you have completed the entire lampshade. As a matter of fact, soldering is something like eating peanuts; once you get started you become more and more proficient; your appetite is whetted and you look for more things to solder. In this instance, your desires will certainly be soon fulfilled because when you have completed soldering the outside of the lampshade, you may turn the lampshade over and solder the entire inside.

The removal of the lampshade from the form is a rather delicate operation, and considerable care must be exercised to insure that the lampshade will retain its shape until the second soldering is accomplished on the inside of the shade.

Figure 10-16. Preparing for the electrical work.

Applying the Electrical and Hanging Hardware

Use a piece of lead came shaped like the letter "U" with legs 1/4" long around the rim of the aperture at the top of the shade. Solder it into place, and then solder it continuously to the lampshade, and also cover the lead came with solder just as you have covered the copper foil with solder. This is called the aperture ring, and provides a relatively larger surface for applying the vase cap to the lampshade.

Applying the Antiquing Solution

At this point it is important to clean the lampshade completely. One of the simplest ways is to apply whiting in small quantities to the lampshade and brush the lampshade with a stiff bristled brush. The whiting is a very absorbent material, and will pick up all of the flux which has dripped onto the glass, and also act as a polishing agent to polish the metal and the glass. Next, apply a small quantity of sawdust and go over the lamp again with a stiff bristled brush, followed by more sawdust and a rag made from an old towel with plenty of nap.

The copper sulphate solution should then be applied to all of the exposed metals using a small brush such as an artists' camel-hair paintbrush. This copper sulphate solution if used properly will darken the metal down to the proper tone, after which the excess can be removed with soap and water or the entire lampshade can be put into a bathtub or sink and flushed with plain water. The lampshade should then be dried using clean rags.

Figure 10-17. Applying the antiquing solution.

CHAPTER 11

A 1,000-PIECE LAMPSHADE USING THE COPPER FOIL METHOD

Figure 11-1. This copy of the Grape Trellis Shade by Tiffany Studios contains large amounts of "Plating" which is discussed in this chapter.

Using the copper foil method has demonstrated its great adaptability for unlimited design possibilities in lampshade work. Now that you have mastered the skills in working with copper foil and applying them to a form, and have seen how a relatively simple lampshade can be constructed, you may direct your attention to an extremely complicated and delicate project. This project may take several months of spare time work, but when it is completed, it will be a very valuable lampshade, both from a standpoint of time and materials and when considered as a work of art.

We do not intend that you should copy the design used in this chapter. In order to demonstrate the technique however, it is necessary to have a design basis.

This lampshade is based on an original Tiffany lampshade called The Grape Trellis. It measures 26" from corner to corner, and 25" from side to opposing side. At its highest point it is 10 1/2" high. It has a 4" aperture. It is octagonal and has a 4" apron or skirt.

The Grape Trellis shade depicts a grapevine which is in various stages of development. The color scheme in the original is dramatic. The small leaves are either dark green or a white streaked lighter green. As the leaves increase in size, their colors change to yellow green and finally, in the foliage which is past prime, brownish green predominates. The yellowish stems intertwine throughout the shade, sometimes over the lattice and quite often under them. The grapes vary from a deep purple into gradations of reddish, streaked with hints of other colors to depict grapes which are not quite ripe.

The Form

Instead of constructing a solid form for this lampshade, we will construct a form made of heavy corrugated cardboard (smooth on both sides) such as the type used in shipping cartons. They can usually be obtained at grocery stores. This form will be used only for assembling the flat panels of the shade, rather than as a working form.

You can use the dimension given for the pattern to construct the form. The form consists of 8 flat pieces of cardboard each, of 4 different shapes. This totals 32 pieces; one half of which are narrow strips depicting the grape trellis and one half of which are the flat sections of the shade.

Use a very sharp knife, or preferably a razor blade to cut each part of the form separately. You have eight different patterns for the eight sides of the shade. Each of these eight patterns are divided into four sub-sections. You should make a separate piece

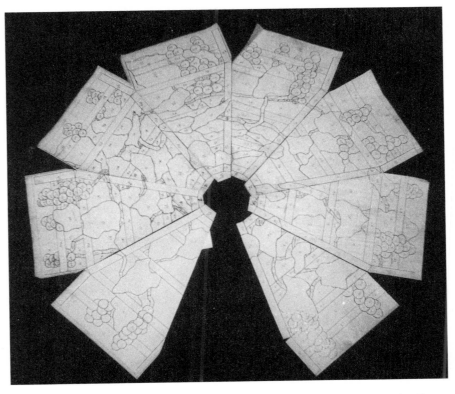

Figure 11-2. Checking contiguous portions of the pattern against each other.

75

of cardboard for each of these four sub-sections, so that when you finish you have 32 pieces of cardboard. Two of the pieces of cardboard will be narrow strips, representing the trellis. One of the pieces will be a skirt panel, and one of the pieces will be the trapezoid which makes the panel for the top. Use extreme accuracy in making these cardboard panels, because these are the basic forms on which the glass panels will be built. When you have them all cut out, use masking tape to assemble them into the shape of the form. Using any sequence you prefer, make sure that the edges of the pieces of cardboard contact each other on the surfaces that will be facing the outside of the form. When we constructed our form, we assembled all of the cardboard together in the same manner that the patterns are assembled together in figure number 11—2. We taped all of the seams with masking tape, and then did all of our bending as a final step. In this way, we insured that the outer surface of the form was exactly the same size as the patterns. In any event, after you have got the form completed and taped on the outer surface, you should also tape the inside seams to add strength.

The Pattern

Our pattern is a grape trellis, but you may prefer designing your own pattern. If you decide to do this, you should first make a complete master pattern consisting of 32 panels for the entire shade. They should be assembled the way they are shown in figure 11—2, and taped together lightly while the design is being drawn. There are several possibilities of designs in this lampshade shape, such as floral design incorporating vines, variations of the grape trellis, or even a geometrical design.

In any event, your design work must be done while the pattern sections are connected together so that the design can carry over between the panels.

Our instructions throughout the chapter will be predicated upon the design of the Grape Trellis as we have shown it, and you must understand that any statements we make should be modified if they apply to another design.

The pattern for this lampshade is neither a working drawing nor a stencil. Do not cut it up and do not work upon it. Instead, using heavy brown paper, trace two copies of all of the patterns. Wherever a straight line occurs, use a ruler so that your traced straight line is actually straight. While you have your original drawing tacked in place over the two copies, trace the color code as well as a location code number. This location code number should designate the panel in which the piece occurs, and the number of the piece. Example: A1, A2, A3, A4, etc. for the first panel. After you have finished tracing the panel, every piece indicated on the pattern should have a designation for color code, and a designation for piece number.

Repeat this procedure for all eight of the pattern sections, and when you have finished, take the pattern for panel #1 and begin cutting out the first copy (the most legible one) with an "Exacto" razor knife, using a straight edge for all straight lines and preferably a swivel razor knife for all curves. (Figure 11—3.) (Note: We refer to the first brown paper copy, not the original copy.)

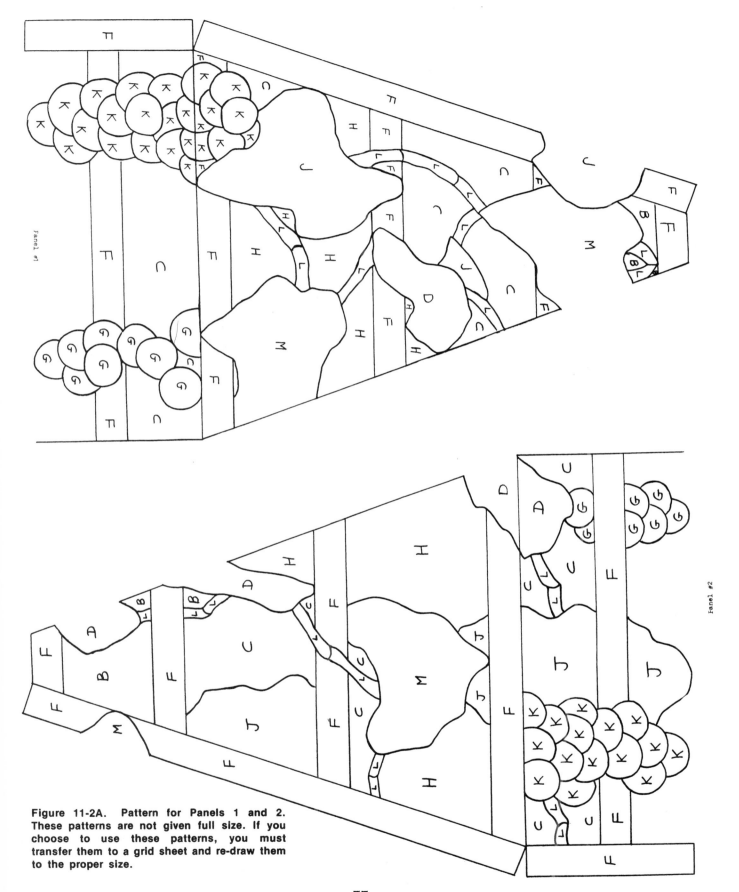

Figure 11-2A. Pattern for Panels 1 and 2.
These patterns are not given full size. If you
choose to use these patterns, you must
transfer them to a grid sheet and re-draw them
to the proper size.

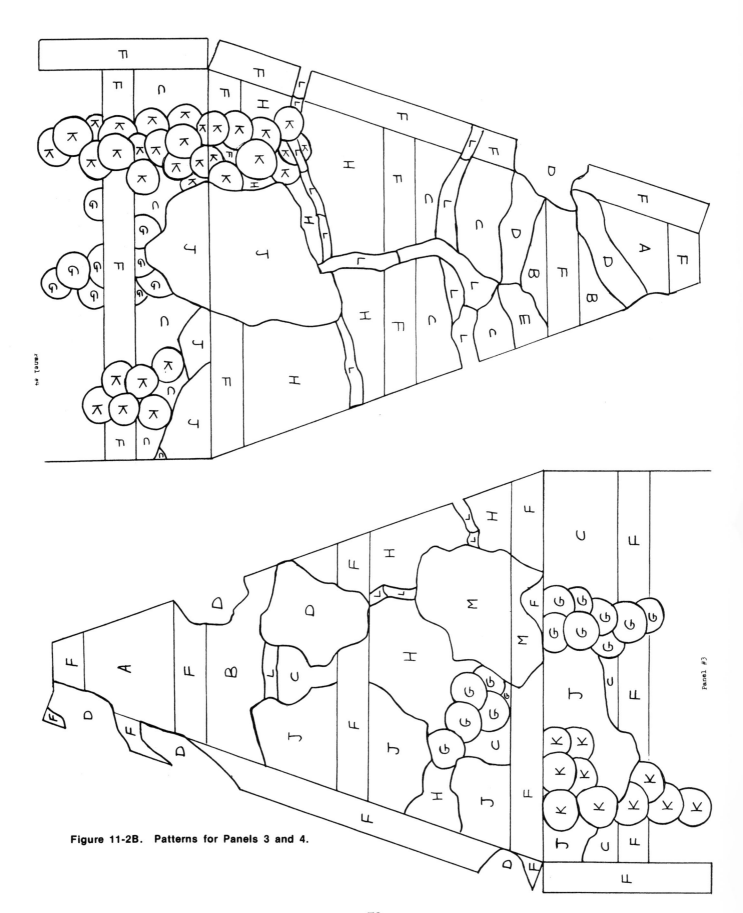

Figure 11-2B. Patterns for Panels 3 and 4.

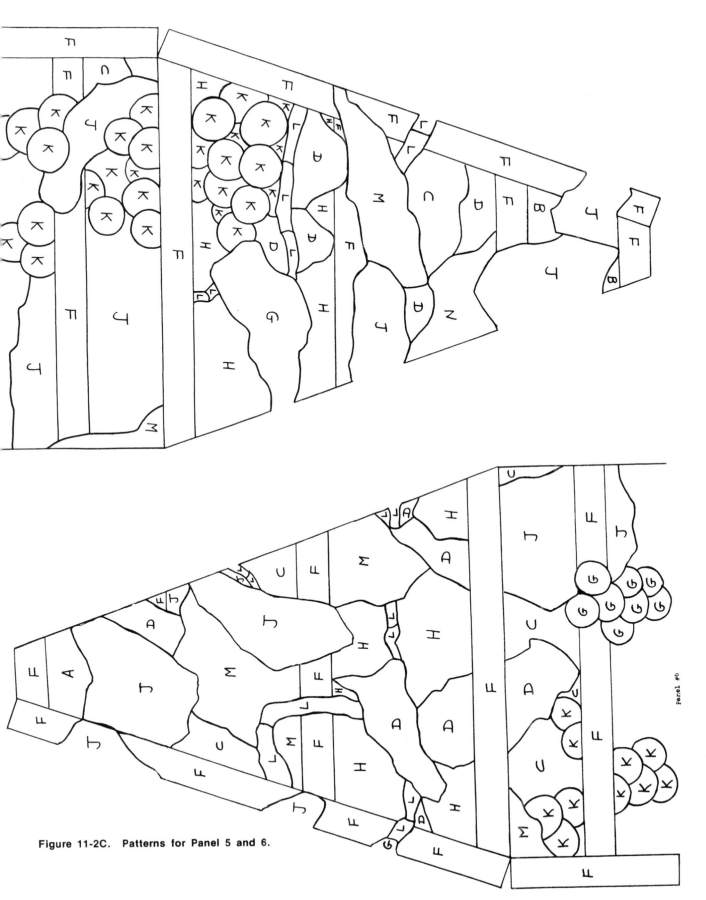

Figure 11-2C. Patterns for Panel 5 and 6.

79

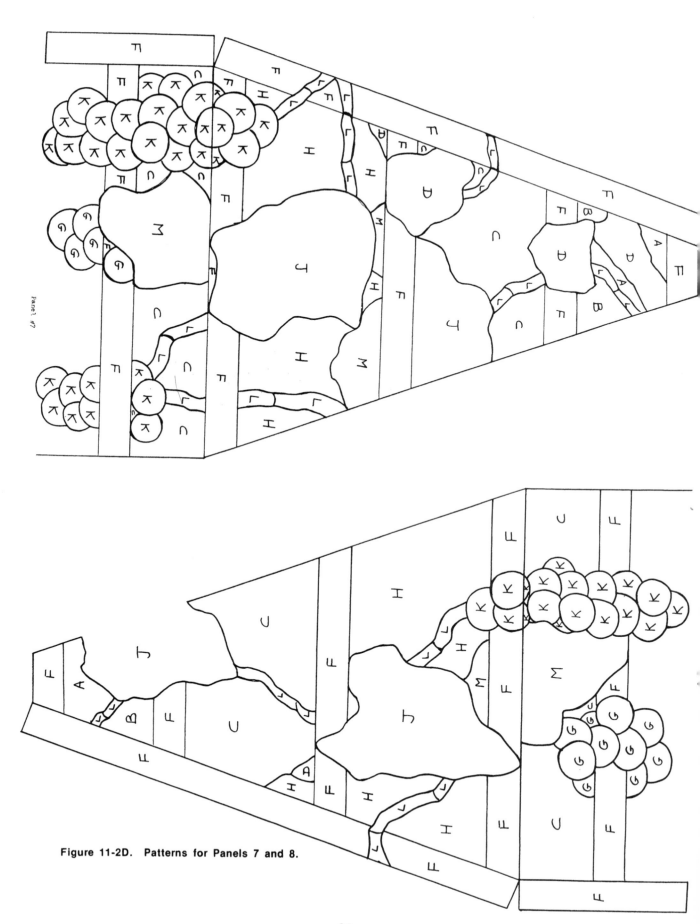

Figure 11-2D. Patterns for Panels 7 and 8.

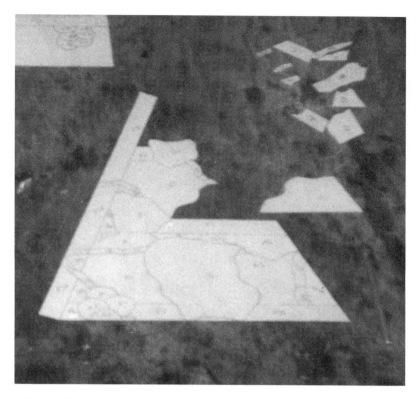

Figure 11-3. Cutting stencils from one of the copies of the pattern.

You should store these various stencils in separate envelopes. Note that each pattern section we have given you contains four separate sub-sections which, if you refer to the photograph, you will note are on separate planes of the shade. You have a large trapezoid section which is 9 5/8 inches wide at the bottom, and 1 1/4 inches wide at the top. You also have a narrow strip which is 3/4 inch wide and 12 3/8 inches high. You also have a skirt section which is 9 5/8 inches wide by 4 inches high as well as a strip section in the skirt which is 3/4 inch wide by 4 inches high. Keep these stencils in four separate envelopes for each of the eight sections of the lampshade. (You will therefore have 32 envelopes when the stencil cutting is complete.)

Cutting The Glass

In order to get the delicate nuances of color and the exact shade desired to depict the various stages of development of the leaves and the grapes, some method must be used to augment the normal palette of glasses available for lampshade work.

Hundreds upon hundreds of glasses were made to order at the Tiffany furnaces at Corona, New York, for their own studio. These glasses covered an extremely wide range of color, surface texture and density. In the work rooms devoted to lampshade making, it was not unusual for craftsmen to cut up large sheets of glass in order to select just the proper piece to use in any given instance. This is not to say that the rest of the sheet was discarded, but we do know that the palette was so extensive that no difficulty was ever encountered in selecting just the proper kind and color of glass.

81

In order to augment our meager palette, we must resort to other means. In this lampshade, which is designed to be an exhibition of fine workmanship, we had best give considerable thought to glass selection early in the design.

During the latter part of the nineteenth century and the early part of the twentieth century, a practice developed which became quite common in window work and to some extent in lampshade work. The practice was called "Plating". This term came to mean the superimposing of one or more pieces of glass over other pieces to change the density of the color, to affect the light transmissions, to add a different texture to a glass which is available in only one texture, or to combine two colors to produce a third color.

We designed our lampshade so that more than three-quarters of the glass in the lampshade required plating.

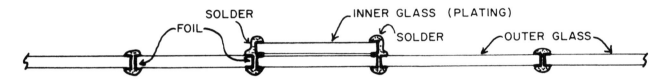

Figure 11-4. Method of attaching "Plating".

Our instructions refer to plating throughout. If you do not care to use plating, or if you have designed a lampshade which does not require any great variation of color shades or richness of color, you will not need to use plating.

Whichever method you use, the surface glass must first be cut for the entire lampshade.

Accuracy here is a must. Beginning with your first envelope, sort the stencils by surface color and begin cutting the glass. Cut only the surface glass at this time. The usual procedure is to cut the color with the smallest quantity first. The logical sequence is to cut the largest pieces first so that the smallest pieces can be cut from scrap. (Note: The second, or underneath glass called "plating" will be cut later.)

Take particular care to position the grain of the variegations in opalescent glass or streakies to follow the natural lines of the leaves, or arrange the grain to simulate the grain in the wood of the trellis or the veins of the stalk of the vine. A little extra care at this point will add considerably to the final over-all effect yet cost nothing. You will note that many of the pieces of glass for this shade contain inward curves, some very extreme. The best way to cut them is by "grozing" out. This amounts to nibbling with your pliers, to chew the notch or inward curve required. None of these difficult cuts should be attempted with one swipe of course. When you come to a piece of glass that overlaps onto the verticals slats of the trellis to the left or to the right, do not cut these pieces at this time. Clip the paper pattern to the outside of your envelope for cutting later.

Because of the amount of pieces and the exactness required, it is almost necessary to grind the edges of the glass so it is exact with the individual stencil. A small bench grinder can be used, or a small stone attached to an electric drill. A very slow speed is required, and extreme care must be used if you decide to do any grinding. Pieces of glass can be impelled from the wheel, and goggles should be worn.

The glass should be stacked or accumulated on the second copy of your pattern sheet. This will insure that the glass is being cut correctly and the pieces will interlock as required. It will also check on the bookkeeping of the work, and disclose immediately if a stencil has been lost.

Glazing

Begin wrapping all glass for panel number 1 with copper foil. Use 3/16ths foil wherever possible, to give the finer sightline desired. As you wrap the glass with copper foil, place it onto copy #2 of the pattern (your working drawing) to make sure it fits exactly. (Figure 11-5.) If any adjusting needs to be done, this is the time to do it. It would be better to recut pieces of glass at this juncture, than to have a lampshade with large areas of solder filled in to correct sloppy cutting. Remember that when your lampshade is illuminated, all of the soldering and all of the metalwork is shown in silhouette and you should strive for the least amount of outline, and attempt to have as delicate a tracery as possible. Continue to assemble the pieces until you have all of the pieces for panel #1 in place on the working drawing.

Figure 11-5. Locating the glass pieces on the copy of the pattern to check the accuracy of the cutting.

When everything has been adjusted to your satisfaction, take an artist's brush and apply your oleic acid flux to all of the copper surfaces showing. (Figure 11-6.)

Begin your soldering operation by spot-soldering at strategic areas to hold all the pieces firm. (Figure 11-7.) You may wish to use nails to keep all of the pieces in position while you are getting started. After you have spot-soldered at the areas needed, go back and do the finish soldering. **Remember to do the four sub-sections separately.** Do not solder them together! When you have finished one panel of the pattern, you should have four separate areas, namely: A trapezoid, a skirt section, a short trellis piece, and a long trellis piece. After you have soldered the complete upper surface of one of these sub-sections, turn it over and do the other side. Put a thin coat of solder on all copper surfaces, but don't over-do it. This is so the plating will sit properly. If you "bead up" the solder on the underside, the plating will not be as close to the other piece of glass as you would like.

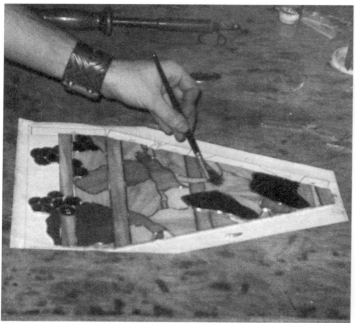

Figure 11-6. Applying the flux preparatory to soldering.   Figure 11-7. Spot-soldering to hold the pieces in place.

Plating

(The following part of the instructions will not be necessary if you have elected to use the glass in a single layer rather than to plate it.)

Cut all the pieces of glass for the so-called "plating" using the same cut-out patterns as you used before. The same exactness is necessary for cutting the glass for the plating. As you go along, place the corresponding plating on the finished original section to make sure they fit. Do not wrap the plating in copper foil and do not solder them to the section yet. This will come after all sections are assembled on the form. Put the plating in a small box and set it aside till later. It would be a good idea to identify each piece of the glass you have cut by a crayon mark on it, or by keeping the paper pattern in the box with the glass. There are many similar pieces of glass, and unless you sort and resort as you go along, you spend a lot of time unnecessarily trying to identify loose pieces of paper and glass.

Completing the Glazing Operation

Repeat the first steps given above for glazing and plating on all the succeeding sections until all of the panels are assembled, and all the plating glass is cut and put into boxes.

Assembling the Shade

The assembly of this lampshade will be different than the assembly of any of the other lampshades in the book, and will illustrate again the various techniques possible in lampshade making. The lampshade form you have constructed out of cardboard will be the basis of the assembly.

84

Figure 11-8. Assembling the lampshade upon the cardboard form.

To begin soldering the sections onto the form use nails or pins to hold the upper portion of the lampshade panels into place. Begin with a trapezoid, and place the corresponding vertical trellis piece next to it, hold it in place with pins or nails, and spot-solder it to the trapezoid. Put your next trapezoid piece in place, hold it in a similar manner with nails, spot solder it to the adjacent piece, add the next vertical trellis piece and proceed this way around the eight sides of the shade. (Figure 11-8.) At the last spot, connect the #8 section to the #1 section by spot-soldering it. When everything is lined up correctly, go back and solder the trapezoids together permanently. When this is completed, you are ready to cut the glass that overlaps. Begin by placing a piece of tag board or thin cardboard made from a manilla folder, under the glass (that is between the glass panel and the form). Trace around the opening, remove the tag board, and cut out the pattern. Use this pattern to cut the overlap glass rather than the pattern that was cut out originally. The reason we suggest this is that due to the bending of the panels, there is a slight distortion and the pattern you will make in the manner described above will be more accurate. Wrap this piece of glass in foil and solder it in place in the opening. You will note that the left and right ends of this glass will be raised up above the plane of the other glass surrounding it. This is alright as long as you are able to fill up the joint between the adjacent pieces of copper with solder. If there is any difficulty, try to depress this piece of glass below the surface of the adjacent glass so you will be able to fill the joint around the perimeter with solder. Proceed with all of your overlap glass in a similar manner.

Now place the corresponding skirt sections onto the form, and solder them to the top. They may be held in place with spring type clothes pins or with pins and nails as

85

before. Be patient, because at this point you cannot tilt up the form to solder it. After the shade is complete, you will be able to go over all the seams and smooth them, but at this point, you may find some difficulty in spot-soldering on a vertical surface.

Securing the Top

After the skirt is soldered into place, you must secure the top opening with "U" channel lead. Place lead completely around the edge of the opening and solder it at all points to the copper foil seams. For extra strength it is advised that you tin the lead with solder, which means to flow the solder continuously over the lead just as you do with the copper foil. Do this only after the lead is completely in place.

Figure 11-9. Using the cardboard lampshade form as an outer support whilst working on the inside of the shade.

Soldering the Insides of the Seams

Carefully lift the shade off the form. **Do not turn it over.** Place it to one side. Tie a string around the skirt near the lower edge. This will keep the skirt from spreading, which you will see is possible when you read the subsequent steps. Slit the tape of the skirt section of the cardboard form along the vertical joints, (the 4 inch dimension). Turn the form over, and then turn the lampshade over, and place the lampshade inside of the form. You will note that to give additional support to the lampshade during this episode, we have tied a string around the perimeter of the skirt. It would be a good idea to have one or two other persons to help you do this part of the action, because the shade is in a very weak condition. Place the shade inside the form upside down as shown in the photograph. (Figure 11-9.) When the shade is in the form, retape the skirt portion of the form and with the shade supported in this fashion, solder all of the seams of the entire shade together on the inside, in the same way that you soldered the outside. Remember to put only a thin tinning coat on the copper, because you will be adding plating to this area, and large globs or hunks of solder will be in the way.

Adding the Plating

Begin by wrapping all of the plating for all of the sections with copper foil. Before soldering the plating, clean all of the surfaces of the glass on the inside of the shade to be sure that all the pieces of solder or debris have been removed, because once we have attached the plating it will be too late to remove them.

Begin plating section #1, by placing the first piece of plating onto the corresponding piece of glass beneath it, and soldering around the perimeter of the plating piece to attach it to the copper below it. Solder all of the edges where one piece of plating will butt up against another piece of plating, because it would be unneccessary here. Where two pieces butt together, just solder them together normally. Be careful that the solder doesn't flow between the glass. When you have attached all of the plating, turn the shade over, and place it at a tilt to finish soldering the skirt joints together.

Antiquing the Metalwork

We have shown in other chapters the methods and materials used for applying the antique look to the metalwork. The one variation from this process which would apply to

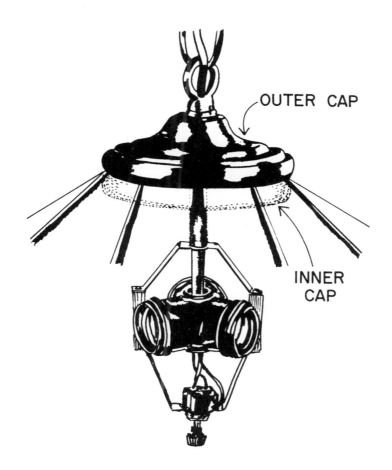

OUTER CAP

INNER CAP

Figure 11-10. Suggested wiring and hanging arrangement.

this particular lampshade would apply only if plating is used. If you have plated the lampshade you cannot use antiquing solution in large quantities because it might run between the glasses that are plated, in which case it would be impossible to remove. Due care must be given in this instance, or a problem might arise.

Cleaning the Shade

The same caution would apply in cleaning the shade. It would be better to use something like Windex, or a commercial cleaner used for cleaning glass rather than anything involving large amounts of liquid because of the danger of having the liquid run between the plating. In any event the whole shade should be cleaned inside and out, and the earlier the better. The flux and the antiquing solution have a way of becoming more difficult to remove the longer they have been allowed to set.

Summary

We have attempted to show an extremely complicated lampshade project encompassing almost all of the problems one would encounter in building the most involved lampshade. More difficult projects are undoubtedly possible, but the basic steps involved would be no more than the ones shown in this chapter. Accuracy in cutting the glass is the prime prerequisite in this or any other lampshade with hundreds of interlocking pieces.

CHAPTER 12

HANGING AND ELECTRICAL HARDWARE

Figure 12-1. Typical electrical and hanging hardware application.

Hanging or Mounting the Lampshade

In general, lampshade mountings can be divided into two groups. They are either for use on a stand or lamp base, or they are designed for hanging from a ceiling or bracket. The hardware used for each have several components in common, but some of the hardware is quite different. We will discuss the types of hardware available for mounting your lampshade, and attempt to clarify the differences and the appropriateness of the various types.

1. Hardware for Hanging a Lamp

Almost all lampshades which are suspended are done so through the use of a chain. The chain acts as a supporting device to suspend the lampshade from a hook or other fixture in the ceiling or, in some instances, from a bracket. The electrical cord is quite often intertwined with the chain, but does not bear any of the weight.

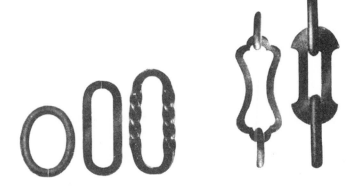

Figure 12-2. Some interesting designs of chains.

The popularity of hanging lamps and so-called "swag lamps" has increased so much in recent years that an entire new segment of the chain manufacturing industry has developed which caters to this class of trade. There are literally hundreds of kinds of chains available for hanging a lamp. The sizes and shapes of the links vary to such an extent that it would be impossible to describe them, and the most we can do is to give some illustrations. To further confuse the situation, there is a very large variety of finishes and platings available.

There is literally a chain for every mood and for every occasion. Fortunately, the stained glass craftsman can limit himself to a certain narrow group of choices.

Inasmuch as many of the lampshade projects are complemented nicely by the use of an antiquing solution on the metalwork of the shade, it follows that a chain with an antique brass or pewter finish would seem most suitable.

Figure 12-3. Several kinds of loops.

Methods of Attaching the Chain to the Lampshade

In almost all instances the chain is attached to the lampshade by a loop. This is usually a brass casting, or a steel or zinc casting which has been brass plated. The loop not only provides a place to attach the chain, but it has a hole through its base through which the lampcord can be passed. This hole is important, because it is the aperture through which the cord can enter into the lampshade. The part of the loop which fits against the top of the lampshade is tapped to receive the threaded pipe, or nipple which passes down through the top of the lampshade into the inside where the electrical parts are attached.

Depending upon the design of the lampshade, or whether the lampshade has a glass "crown", the lampshade may or may not have an elaborate or functional cap. The usual cap for a hanging lampshade is called a vase cap. It is a bowl-shaped spinning or stamping of either brass or plated steel, with a hole in it large enough to pass or slip the threaded pipe. The vase cap can be treated with the same antique solution with which the metalwork of the shade is treated, or it can be sprayed with any of a variety of copper or dull brass lacquers to make it blend better with the metalwork of the shade.

Figure 12-4. A vase cap.

Some vase caps are quite elaborate and decorative. In stained glass work, the usual practice, however, is to use a plain vase cap to avoid detracting from the central point of interest, the lampshade itself.

When there is a crown of glass around the top of the shade the vase cap is usually not used, but a fixture strap is used instead. The fixture strap is soldered to the edge of the aperture of the shade, and the threaded pipe is screwed through the hole in the center of the fixture strap. The loop is then screwed onto the portion of the threaded pipe which protrudes through the strap.

Figure 12-5.   A fixture strap, sometimes called a "Cross bar."

The fixture strap is most commonly unplated steel. It is rarely visible when a hanging shade is mounted, and most craftsman do not attempt to apply an antique finish or similar treatment to it. If a fixture strap is used, other hardware seldom is used inside the shade other than the electrical hardware.

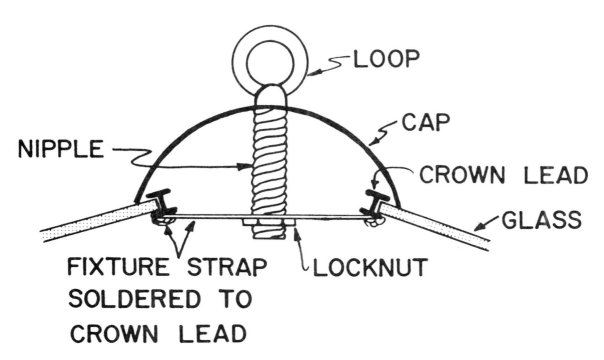

Figure 12-6.   Suggested arrangement using a cross bar and a vase cap for hanging a lamp.

If a vase cap is used, however, some other device must be used just beneath the aperture of the shade to carry the weight of the lampshade. The vase cap is no more than a decorative piece of hardware.

In some instances, a second vase cap is used inside the shade. The inner and outer vase caps which are both larger in diameter than the aperture form a "sandwich" which supports the lampshade.

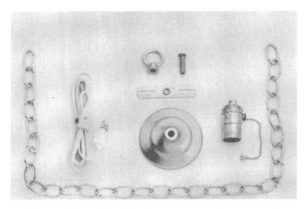

Figure 12-7. The hardware required to mount a lamp in the manner shown in figure 12-6.

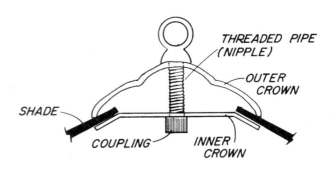

Figure 12-8. The use of an inner and outer vase cap for hanging a lampshade.

Variations of the above hanging methods do occur. One of the major variations is in the length of the chain. There are assemblies consisting of chains and cords 15 feet long which are called "Swag Lamp Kits". The lampshade is hung from a hook in the ceiling. A second hook is put into the ceiling as closely to the wall as possible. The chain is then hung from the first hook and festooned across the ceiling to the second hook. It is then dropped down the wall. The cord, which is intertwined with the chain, is plugged into a convenience outlet on the wall.

Figure 12-9. The hardware required to mount and electrify [with two bulbs] a lampshade as shown in figure 12-8.

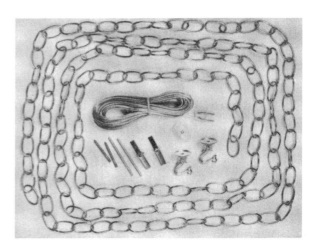

Figure 12-10. "Swag" type hardware consisting of 15 feet of cord and chain.

This type of hanging arrangement has the advantage of being very versatile. The lamp can be suspended from almost any point in the ceiling, provided the chain will reach from that point to the convenience receptacle.

Other variations include the use of a ceiling cap, which is fitted with a hook. A ceiling cap is a device which is fastened to the ceiling outlet. The lampshade is hung from a hook in the cap. The cap also has a receptacle into which the cord can be plugged. This arrangement has the advantage of being controlled through the wall switch that originally controlled the ceiling outlet.

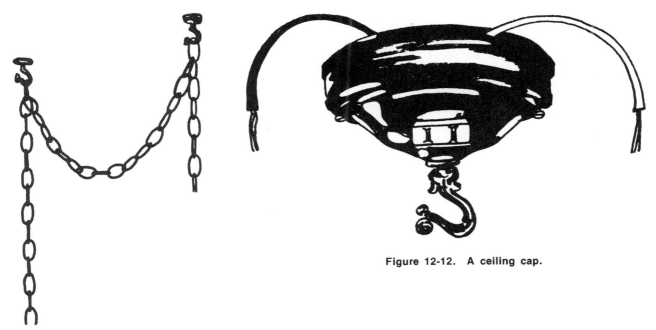

Figure 12-12. A ceiling cap.

Figure 12-11. Application of swag hardware.

Other variations of the hanging type hardware include brackets which can swivel, and devices for hanging several small lamps from the same bracket.

2. Hardware for Mounting onto a Lamp Base

Reading lamps, table lamps and stand lamps quite often have similar devices for accommodating the lampshade. This device usually consists of a stud or threaded bolt over which the lampshade is slipped. The shade is held in place by a finial piece which is usually a brass casting or plated steel casting with an internal thread to screw onto the stud.

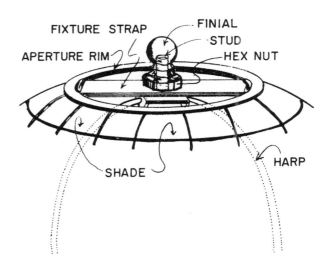

Figure 12-13. Using a fixture strap to mount a lampshade on a harp.

Lampshades to be used thusly must be equipped with some device across the aperture hole to accept the stud. The usual way to handle this is to use a fixture strap. If the stud is smaller than the hole in the fixture strap, a washer and nut is run onto the stud to hold the lamp from wobbling. After the fixture strap is attached to the lamp base, a vase cap is put over the top of the lamp, covering the aperture and all of the hardware and held in place with a finial which is screwed down onto the stud (which in most cases is long enough to protrude up through the vase cap).

Another way of handling the mounting of a lampshade onto a lamp base is to use an inner and outer vase cap. These vase caps must be soldered to the lampshade. A nut can be put onto the stud, and the lampshade dropped onto the stud so that it rests on the nut. A finial can then be screwed down onto the portion of the stud which protrudes up through the hole in the vase cap thus securing the lampshade and preventing it from wobbling.

In the chapter on lamp bases we will show various ways of arranging the electrical hardware on the lamp base.

3. Electrical Hardware

The method of electrifying lampshades varies somewhat from craftsman to craftsman, but is also somewhat bound by necessity and tradition. Almost certainly, every lampshade must have a lampcord and a socket into which a light bulb may be screwed.

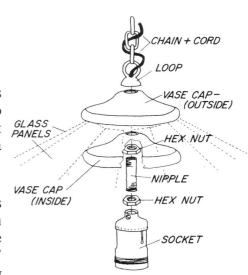

Figure 12-14. A typical electric lay-out for most leaded glass production-type lampshades.

A typical hanging lampshade might be electrified as follows: The threaded pipe which protrudes down through the top of the shade and which was described in the earlier part of this chapter under "Hanging Hardware" may be continued downward as far as desired by adding couplings and more threaded pipes. When the desired length is reached, a socket can be attached to the end of the pipe. A hex nut is used as a stop against which to screw the socket. This hex nut will prevent the socket from turning when bulbs are screwed in and out of the socket. The lamp cord is fed into the lampshade by threading it through the chain, through the cast loop at the top of the shade and down through the threaded pipe into the socket. The attachments are made inside of the socket, and the lampshade is ready for use. (See Figure 12-14.)

Multiple Sockets

If the lampshade is a very large one, it may be desirable to use more than one bulb. If this is so, various devices called "cluster bodies" are available which can be attached to the end of the primary pipe, and from out of which other threaded pipes can be run. Cluster bodies are available to accommodate anywhere from two to six outlets. Short pieces of lamp cord must be cut and spliced together to make all of the connections needed within the cluster body to bring current out to the various sockets which are attached to other threaded pipes which feed into the cluster body.

There are other devices available for accomplishing the work of the cluster body. These are of various quality and some care must be used in choosing them so that they do not detract from the general quality of the work.

Electrification of Lamp Bases

Inasmuch as the electrical part of the hardware does not attach to the lampshade when a lamp base is being used, we will refer the reader to the chapter on lamp bases where the electrification of bases is covered. If a lampshade is to be used on a lamp base, no other electrical work is required on the lampshade.

4. Miscellaneous Hardware for Hanging and Electrifying Lampshades

The following hardware is also used in lampshade work and a brief description is given on the function of it.

Figure 12-15.   A cluster body which is used for joining two or more sockets into the main electrical source.

Figure 12-17.   An angle nozzle which is used to bring the wires out of the cluster body at an angle so the socket and bulb will be held down from the lampshade.

Figure 12-19. A finial used on top of a vase cap when the lampshade is mounted on a lamp base.

Figure 12-16. A hex nut, which is threaded to fit over the threaded pipe.

Figure 12-18.   A coupling for joining two threaded pipes.

Figure 12-20. A threaded pipe or nipple. These come in an endless variety of sizes.

CHAPTER 13

LAMP BASES

We have treated this subject separately from other hanging and electrical hardware because of the distinction between them. A lamp base is a separate piece of equipment or apparatus which at most is fastened mechanically to the lampshade. This differs from the hardware used when a lamp is hung, which is often soldered to the lampshade, or at the very least becomes a permanent part of the shade.

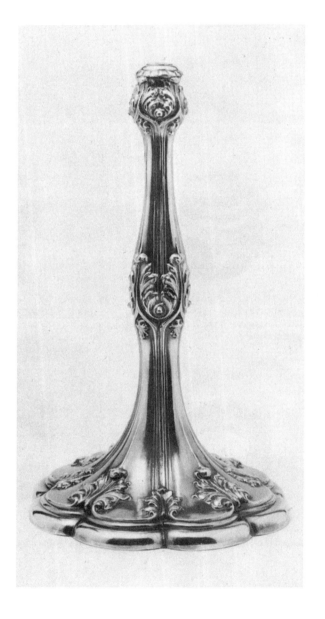

Figure 13-1. Simple lines and fine details are requirements for any lamp base to be used with a stained glass shade.

Figure 13-2. Lamp Bases made from white metal present the greatest opportunity for various types of surface treatments.

Despite the fact that the lampshade is a separate item, it must be chosen with care and must entirely reflect the theme and style of the lampshade which is to be mounted upon it.

Considerations to be given when choosing a lamp base are as follows:

A. The Size. No rule of thumb can be given here, but obviously there is some leeway in size range which makes it impossible to set forth a hard and fast rule as to the ratio between the height of the lamp base and the diameter of the shade. If possible, the shade should be tried on the lamp base before purchasing it. If this is not possible, a quick sketch drawn to scale of the lampshade and lamp base may reveal something of the finished appearance.

B. Style. Here again no hard and fast rule can be applied, but modernistic lamp bases certainly cannot be considered as stands for lampshades in the style of the Victorian era. The same holds true for Colonial designs, such as wrought iron, etc. Other inappropriate designs may come to mind.

C. Material. Most preferences are for metal lamp bases, cast from brass, white metal, or iron. They have the weight required to give a firm foundation, which is required to prevent the lamp from being easily upset. The finishes on the metals can vary from brass plating, or platings of other kinds which may be augmented or modified by the application of antiquing solutions. These antiquing solutions may be of the chemical type, or may be surface treatments based on paint or lacquer. Generally speaking, the usual practice is to apply some sort of patina giving the illusion of great age.

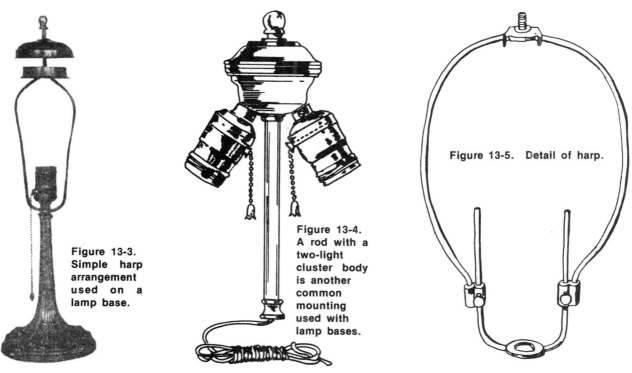

Figure 13-3. Simple harp arrangement used on a lamp base.

Figure 13-4. A rod with a two-light cluster body is another common mounting used with lamp bases.

Figure 13-5. Detail of harp.

Electrifying the Lamp Base. If you have purchased a lamp base from an antique store or a used furniture store, most of the electrical work is intact. You may have to replace the lamp cord and possibly the socket. If you are purchasing a new lamp base, however, which you intend to electrify on a custom basis, you will need to consider the following points.

a. The Mounting Device for the Lampshade. There are several ways to attach the lampshade to the lamp base. Each of them has certain advantages, and their choice quite often depends on the size and shape of the lampshade. Some of these possibilities are shown. The harps come in many sizes. Needless to say, the rod can also be used in many different sizes.

Figure 13-6. Intricate root-like lamp base designed specifically for a leaded glass shade. This lampshade is 21" in diameter.

Figure 13-7. A 16" diameter shade on an attractive base.

b. The Cord. Most lamp bases have a hole near the base through which the cord may pass to run through the cavity of the lampshade and come through the top opening. Lamp bases with legs or bases with uneven bearing plates may not have this hole because the cord can pass beneath the shade. If the socket in the shade is to be equipped with a chain or a switch, the lamp cord may be of the simple variety that plugs into a convenience outlet. If you prefer to use a keyless socket, however, the lamp cord should have a cord switch. These are available at any electrical store. The lamp cord used in this type work is preferably cloth covered. An antique gold color is attractive.

c. Sockets. As in the hanging shades, it is possible to have more than one socket on the lamp by the introduction of a cluster body. More than one bulb is seldom used however because most reading lamps are relatively small and do not require them. Some of the lampshades using denser glasses, however, may require a wider dispersion of the light, and two or three bulbs of small wattage may be more preferable than one large bulb.

Sources of Lamp Bases. The supply and demand equation has been hard at work in the lampshade base market for a number of years now, and the price of used lampshades bases from the latter nineteenth century and twentieth century has become scarce enough so that prices have been moving up quite steadily.

Figure 13-8. A base that complements the shade.   Figure 13-9. Another attractive lamp base.

Tiffany Studio lamp bases with signature tags attached almost always bring prices in excess of $1,000.00. Being aware of this situation makes the price quotations on other handsome and desirable lampshade bases easier to take. Antique dealers are aware of this market, and a good supply is usually available. The dealers generally get their supply of articles such as this from wholesale antique dealers who have "pickers" who attend auctions of household furniture, and who travel the circuit of used furniture stores in smaller towns in rural areas. By the time the lamp bases arrive to the point where they make their appearance in the store of Mr. Antique Dealer the lamp base may have graduated from being a $4.00 item to become a $40.00 item.

All this points up the fact that if you want to spend enough time and if you have the ingenuity, and most important, if you have the luck, you may uncover a very desirable and valuable lampshade base at an extremely low price. If you do not wish to spend the time and effort, however, you may purchase one.

Used furniture stores, thrift shops, and similar establishments also have lamp bases from time to time. They must be visited regularly, however, and the proprietor or manager should be advised to notify you whenever one turns up.

New Lamp Bases. There are large foundries in some parts of the country which specialize in casting components of many decorative types, some of which are lamp bases. Most of the lamp bases are made in separate sections. Thus, bases and rods, risers and breaks, finials and pedestals can be mixed to obtain special styles.

They will not deal with individuals nor fill orders for small quantities, so the normal chain of distribution for their products is through electrical supply houses or firms specializing in supplies for the stained glass hobbyist.

Figure 13-10. A good lamp base should be inobtrusive.

Figure 13-11. This lamp base balances the 16" diameter lampshade very well.

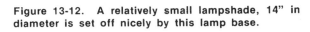

Figure 13-12. A relatively small lampshade, 14" in diameter is set off nicely by this lamp base.

Figure 13-13. There are almost as many lamp base possibilities as there are lampshades.

CHAPTER 14

VARIATIONS

There are several treatments not covered in this book that can be given to stained glass lampshades, and there are also some minor methods of construction techniques which have not been covered. These subjects do not constitute a major departure from the methods and procedures in the various chapters, but any book covering stained glass lampshade construction techniques should include reference to them.

Figure 14-1. A simple modern Lampshade Frame, supplied with simple geometrical panels complements the modernistic lamp base.

Figure 14-2. 16" diameter lamp frame was made in 1915.

A. Lampshade Frames. Many examples of lampshade frames can be seen in reading lamps manufactured between 1880 and 1920. These lampshade frames usually consisted of castings of white metal (which is an alloy of zinc and lead) and before their manufacture was practically discontinued, the design gamut had run from the simply functional to the ornate and rococo.

Figure 14-3. This beautiful lamp frame has a matching lamp base which sets if off very nicely.

Figure 14-4. The ornate 18" frame is set off handsomely by the interesting lamp base.

The general purpose of the frame was so that the glass could be furnished in relatively large pieces, (as few as six). Thus the frame (with all its attendant filigree and decorative work) would be shown in silhouette in front of the glass when the lamp was lighted.

A good many of the lampshade frames were built to accommodate bent glass, but many were designed for flat glass. It is these which are most sought after today. The glass which was originally in them has quite often disappeared by this time, and considerable repair on the frame may be necessary. If you do locate an old frame in a junk store, or second-hand furniture store, do not pass it by. It can be converted into a beautiful lampshade. Some of the beautiful opal and opalescent glasses manufactured today having 3, 4 or 5 colors are very attractive when cut into larger pieces required in a lampshade frame such as this. The glass has a great amount of variation between sections of the sheet, and it is often done better justice in a lampshade such as this, used in fairly large sections than when used in a shade with smaller pieces.

The glass is held in place most often in these lampshade frames by flexible metal clips, usually made of copper, which have been soldered to the frame. They are extremely easy to manipulate, and when you are ready to insert the glass it is a simple matter to clip the glass into the shade.

Figure 14-5. This hexagonal lamp frame is 17" in diameter.

Figure 14-6. This 16" diameter frame has a very interesting pictorial over-lay.

These lampshade frames may also be refinished, repainted or treated in the same way that any similar metalwork may be treated.

The aperture in the frames quite often is 3 or 4 inches across, and to electrify it and to modify it into a hanging lamp may require some ingenuity, but it usually can be accomplished by the use of two vase caps installed in a manner similar to the way the vase caps are sometimes installed in hanging lampshades.

Simple metal lampshade frames are also available newly made. They are very simple devices made of a steel angle welded together. They have wide expanses for glass. They differ from the older type lamp frames in that they are manufactured specifically for the use of leaded glass.

To use them, you make a pattern outline which will fit one of the panels, and design the panel to fit this outline. The glass is then cut into multiples of the quantity needed to make panels for the entire shade. The panels are glazed and soldered on a flat surface, either with lead came or copper foil. The finished panels are clipped into the lampshade frame.

Figure 14-7. This modern lamp frame has been filled with unleaded sheets of opalescent glass. All types of leaded work can be substituted for the opalescent glass if desired.

As you might guess, it is possible to have several sets of panels for a lampshade frame such as this, and change them from time to time as you see fit.

B. Metal Accessories. You may have noticed other material introduced into some stained glass lampshades. One of the materials most often used is metal banding. These bandings may be made of brass, plated steel, or lead. In some instances they are used to cover the joints between panels in a curved shade. In these instances they are soldered to the brass channeling which covers the edge of the glass and which serves as the basis for soldering the panels together. These bandings are also used to form the collar around larger shades, thus covering the joint between the glass crown and the main portion of the shade. When used as a collar, the width of the metal banding is usually 1" wide or more.

The banding is also used as a trim along the bottom edge of many types of shades. When used in this way, the banding is usually in the form of a channel, or used as a cosmetic device to hide a channel which is already there covering up the edge of the lampshade.

When banding is used along the edge of a shade, it is quite often punched to receive hanging ornaments of various types. These hanging ornaments are hooked into the holes which are punched along one edge of the banding.

The lead castings are usually of very high relief, and the brass and steel banding, being rolled, are quite flat.

105

Figure 14-8. This lampshade illustrates the use of banding both as covering for the seams, and as a collar.

Figure 14-9. This lampshade has banding which has holes in it to receive the fringe.

Either of these bandings tend to identify the lampshade as being a production-type affair, rather than as a hand crafted item. Any over-use of bandings should be avoided.

C. Lamp Jewels. Lamp jewels can be grouped into three major classifications. They are: Cast or polished jewels incorporated into the design. Curved or bent glass shapes, (usually of fruit) which are incorporated into the design. Pendant-type jewels used as ornamental work along the edge of the shade.

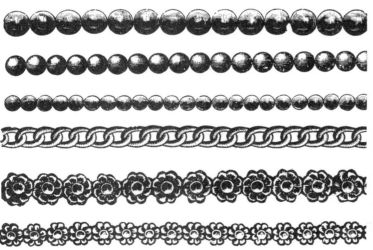

Figure 14-11. A stamped border suitable for a collar.

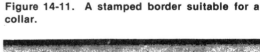

Figure 14-10. The various types of bandings and over-lays used around the turn of the century.

Figure 14-12. A fancy stamped border.

All of these types are very specialized items obtainable only through stained glass craft supply sources. The dies or molds used for any of these type products are expensive, and quantities ordered must be extremely high in order to amortize the cost of the dies and patterns.

I. Cast or Polished Jewels. Cast lampshade jewels were first manufactured during the second half of the nineteenth century. Their early manufacture came about as an off-shoot of the costume jewelry industry.

One of the earliest manufacturers was Leo Popper and Sons of New York City. As late as 1971 the original dies of many of the lampshade jewels were still in existence.

Between the time of the first manufacture of lampshade jewels and the discontinuance, many millions were manufactured. They were made by the Heidt Glass Works, Leo Popper & Sons, and others.

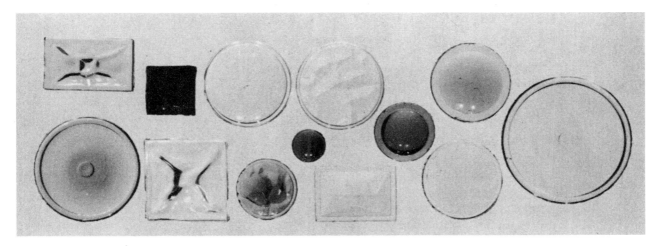

Figure 14-13. Some typical pressed glass lampshade jewels.

107

In addition to the firms which manufactured lamp jewels, there were many other firms making pressed jewels, either faceted or unfaceted, for use in reflectors, signal lenses, and the like. Many of these jewels were identical to some of the lamp jewels, and indeed were used in lampshades.

After the decline of the stained glass lampshade market in the 1920's the manufacture of lampshade jewels declined until it was almost discontinued completely.

There are no domestic firms engaged in the manufacture of lampshade jewels at the present time. They are available, however in moderate supply from abroad. They are being recast from original dies from time to time.

Faceted and unfaceted polished jewels are available through some suppliers because they are used in reflectors and signal lenses as before.

Figure 14-14. Montgomery Ward Company showed this lampshade in their 1915 catalog. It illustrates the use of jewels in a stained glass shade.

The entire series of lampshades called "Dragonfly" shades which were manufactured by the Tiffany Studios utilized oval unfaceted jewels of various colors and various shapes. These all depict droplets of water amongst the general swamplike background. It would be impossible to duplicate this lampshade, should one wish to, without the use of these oval jewels.

This is an illustration of the way the lamp jewels can be used in a design. There are many designs using lampshade jewels. In most cases they are geometrical designs.

It is also possible to make a lampshade entirely from jewels, but most examples seen are very cumbersome because of the amount of metalwork required to fill the spaces between the jewels.

108

II. Bent or Sagged Glass Incorporated into Flat Lampshades.

The most common illustration of this particular treatment is the use of "fruit" which has been made of opalescent glass and then bent in a kiln. These may be apples, pears or other shapes.

Figure 14-15. This lampshade illustrates the use of sagged glass pieces, basically fruits, and also the use of glass jewels for grapes.

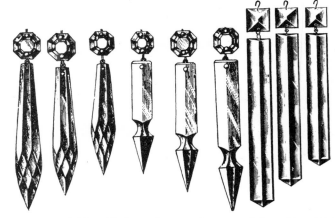

Figure 14-16. Various lamp prisms and hanging ornaments available for lampshade work in the early part of the century.

The effect is to give dimension to the fruit. The location of these items is usually in the skirt of the lampshade.

The over-use of these so-called lampshade fruits immediately identifies the lampshade as being a production lampshade. Before considering the purchase and use of these items, therefore, you should give some thought to the over-all design, and how best these items can be used in it so that the lampshade still maintains the appearance of a custom-made hand-crafted piece.

III. Prisms and Other Hanging Glass Jewels.

In the illustration you will see several types of hanging jewels manufactured for the use in lampshades. To properly use these types of jewels, a provision must be made in the design of the shade for their reception. This usually means that a banding or channel must be used along the bottom edge of the lampshade, and this banding or channel must have holes drilled at regular intervals to receive the wires from the prisms or hanging jewels. There are many terms used to describe these jewels, and the different terms usually refer to the shape of the jewels. Various terms in use are: Prisms, pendalogues, spears, drops, and crystals.

Once again, these jewels must be judiciously used. If utilized on certain fine stained glass lampshades they will inevitably detract from the general over-all effect. Most certainly, long chains of hanging jewels indiscriminately festooned hither and yon beneath a lampshade might be considered by some to be in questionable taste.

D. Fringes. One of the delightful aspects of old lampshades were the cloth fringes supporting the tiny beads which used to dangle from the rim.

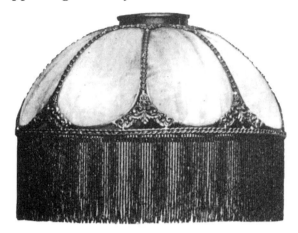

Figure 14-17. Illustrating the use of a beaded fringe on a shade.

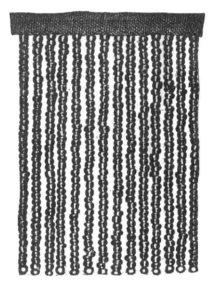

Figure 14-18. Close up of a bead fringe.

Most old lampshades which have been in storage for any length of time have had their fringes consumed by rodents, moths, or other fringe-eating animals. Tastefully used, beaded fringes add a slight plus to certain lampshades. If one is designing one's living room or den in a Byzantine theme, or intends to use the 19th century Hungarian Bordello motif, beaded fringes are de rigueur.

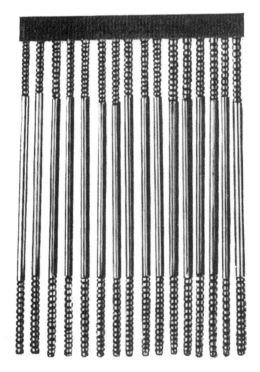

Figure 14-19. Detail of a tube fringe.

Figure 14-20. So-called "Maybelle" fringe.

E. Special Lighting Effects. From time to time it becomes apparent that the use of ordinary dime-store variety bulbs are not exactly what the doctor ordered for a fine stained glass lampshade. One of the difficulties in displaying stained glass lampshades is that many of the opportunities for their use call for them to be suspended from the ceiling a good distance above eye level. When this happens the upper part of the lampshade is not properly seen, but to compound the problem, what **is** seen is the unattractive conglomeration of sockets, pipes, chains, etc. making up the undercarriage of the lamp.

Small clip on diffusers are sold in many electrical stores and in some department stores. These are usually of a neutral appearance, and are made particularly to blend with any design of lampshade. We have seen them used in places where without their use the lampshade would be displayed at a definite disadvantage.

Where this is not feasible, or if you prefer not to introduce extraneous devices into your lampshade, you might prefer using one of the very large globe-type light bulbs which are quite popular.

Another solution might by the use of a globe to cover the bulb. This requires a special fitter which, properly, comes under the heading of electrical work. These globe-type covers are in very common use by production lampshade shops, and for this very reason might best be avoided.

Dimmers and Rheostats. Any lampshade which has required months of part-time work to complete is worth the investment of more time and effort into the consideration of special lighting effects. Many different moods can be generated through the use of different intensities of light when used to illuminate a lampshade. Rather than changing light bulbs frequently, it might be better to equip the lamp with a dimmer apparatus.

Summary. Tastefully used, accessories can add something to a stained glass project, but thoughtful consideration must be given to any decisions along these lines. Adding some Mickey Mouse things to a fine stained glass lampshade which you have designed and executed in the finest tradition of workmanship can have dreadful effects. Anything along these lines is purely a matter of taste, but you must draw the line somewhere.